MARXISM'S STRATEGY FOR DESTROYING AMERICA

DR. RICK JOYNER

MorningStar Publications
www.MorningStarMinistries.org

Marxism's Strategy for Destroying America
By Dr. Rick Joyner

©2021 1st Printing

MorningStar Ministries, Fort Mill, SC. All rights reserved.

**Distributed by MorningStar Publications, Inc.,
a division of MorningStar Fellowship Church
375 Star Light Drive, Fort Mill, SC 29715**

**www.MorningStarMinistries.org
1-800-542-0278**

Cover and layout design: Carlie McKinley

ISBN: 978-1-60708-680-2
For a free catalog of MorningStar Resources, please call 1-800-542-0278

❖ TABLE OF CONTENTS ❖

❖ Chapter 1 ❖

History's Greatest Deception

The Great Enigma

It is generally believed that Nazism is one of the worst evils to ever manifest itself on the planet. We can certainly agree that Nazism is evil, but Marxism has been far worse, many times deadlier than Nazism, and yet tends to get a pass in public opinion. Why?

The simple answer is Marxists have been history's most effective masters of deception. They are so good at deception, they have repeatedly boasted to those they intended to deceive about how they would deceive them, and then destroyed them, just as they said. How have they escaped this with nearly no protest from other nations of the world?

Though Marxists have been the deadliest destroyers of people and civilizations in recorded history, the West not only continues to tolerate Marxism, but they also allow it to be celebrated and even promoted in our schools. Why? These are questions we must answer and act on before the whole world falls into this most deadly black hole.

From the time Karl Marx began to formulate his diabolical doctrines, he declared America his primary target for destruction, then the rest of Western civilization. One of the greatest lessons of history is this: When someone says they want to destroy you, you had better believe them! Yet American and Western leaders have remained shockingly naïve with few exceptions. We have allowed Marxists to get away with murder on a level never witnessed in human history. As Marxists continue to progress toward their stated goal of destroying America and the West, our leaders do little about it. Why?

The answer to this question should have us fundamentally questioning how we choose our leaders if we are to survive these times. The answer to this question will also illuminate the root of many other crises which are now threatening our world. If we do not recognize this soon, and act decisively to counter this ultimate evil, we too, will be destroyed.

Lies vs. Facts

Marxism promises a socialist utopia for all people. Yet it has brought unprecedented suffering, poverty, and depravity everywhere it has gained control. One of the enigmas of history is how a diabolical evil like Marxism, which has proven to come with death and destruction 100% of the time, continues to be esteemed and promoted by anyone much less the nations that are next on its list to subdue. For this reason, this study in Marxism is also a study in deception. If we understand how this ultimate evil has demonstrated such power over reason, it can lead to an understanding of virtually all deceptions.

Now we must understand this evil, because it is close to bringing down the remaining free nations of our world. Perhaps the most remarkable characteristic of this deception is that it is so easy to understand yet almost no one does. It is truly "hiding in plain sight." This indicates a power of deception greater than just mental persuasion.

No one who is deceived knows they are deceived, or they would not be deceived. As deceived as much of the world has been about Marxism and its catastrophic destruction of nations, few believe they are deceived by it. But if not deceived, why do they continue tolerating it? It's like living in a den of cobras and thinking they will be nice to you if you are nice to them.

Recently, several graduate students, who claimed to be socialists studying at one of America's most prestigious universities, were interviewed. Incredibly, not one, who are considered some of America's brightest, could even define socialism! Not fresh out of high school, these were graduate students confidently claiming to be something they could not define! What kind of power is this? It's like our entire nation has been subjected to a Jedi mind trick.

What these graduate students contrived to define socialism made for some good comedy but this is not funny anymore. It is becoming a horror movie and fast. Not only does it reveal how far education in America has been dumbed down, but it is also producing automatons rather than wise, educated future world leaders.

If this is not befuddling, why do so many American academics kneel before Marxist-socialism when they are always the first to be imprisoned or killed when Marxists take over a country? And how does Marxism, the most cruel and diabolical evil of all human scourges, continue to be lauded and promoted in American public education, the media, and arts and entertainment? We must understand this and stand up to this before the whole world becomes the worst of all prisons.

When the Blind Lead

History is filled with mysteries, but this continued toleration of Marxism is the most bizarre. One friend proposed a theory to explain it. He called it "PAC" for "People Are Crazy!" And while that explains many things, the fact that the world still embraces Marxism is the craziest human folly yet, or up there in the top two. This also implies that with all our technological advances and increasing knowledge of our world and of the cosmos, we are not getting any wiser.

Consider that Marxism may be the only movement in history with a message that is entirely based on propaganda without factual basis or truth yet is in fact the opposite of what they promote. This has been clearly demonstrated for over a century and continues to fool even the most powerful and influential people in the world.

When America was founded, people resolved to no longer be ruled by inept, incompetent, or evil governments. Our mission is to recover this resolve and to never again forget it.

Our National DNA

Consider what our Founders accomplished in founding our Republic. To gain freedom, these patriots had to defy the most powerful empire in the world, with the most powerful army and navy in the world, without an army or a single ship! Some states had weak, disorganized militias but these states were not even prone to cooperate with each other. These brave souls faced impossible odds and endured continual defeats for more than five years. Yet they fought on, finally winning their last, biggest battle and their freedom.

However, this miraculous victory led to an even greater challenge—how would they govern this new nation? Each state was unique and independent. To unite to face the many challenges that would come from other nations was essential yet seemingly impossible. Such would require the most inspired, brilliant contract for government the world had ever seen. We call it *The Constitution*. The freedoms it protected released a strength and resolve in its people that resulted in the most powerful and prosperous nation in history.

Will we allow these freedoms that so many paid dearly for to be taken without a fight? I think not. Yet here we are in a place that will require that same kind of courage, resolve, and willingness to sacrifice to save our Republic, as it did to found it.

But first we must understand how Marxism has so easily deceived, subdued, and destroyed so many nations during the time of the world's greatest increase in knowledge. As we pursue an accurate knowledge of Marxism and its strategy for world domination, we must seek the wisdom to know what to do with this knowledge. Then we must find leaders with the courage and resolve to carry this out.

As stated, this is a basic study in Marxism as it has proven to be, not as Marxists claim it to be. It is also a study in deception, including the characteristics and factors that make us vulnerable to deception. In short, it is a study of us. And if we do not soon grasp these things, all this great knowledge we have acquired will be used to make the strongest shackles and yokes ever to be put on humanity. However, if we resolve to understand this great evil and the human folly it has repeatedly created and stand for truth with the courage and resolve it deserves, a new day of freedom may be proclaimed.

It Was All Foretold

Contrary to what atheistic Marxists have indoctrinated into our students and citizens, biblical prophecies have been accurate 100% of the time. Not one has failed. What we are experiencing now can be found in several biblical prophecies and the ultimate outcome is declared. Biblical prophecies repeat that the end of this age will be the greatest time of trouble the world has ever experienced. Yet this is not the "end of the world," rather a new beginning for the world. According to these prophecies, these troubles will lead to the greatest time of peace and prosperity the world has ever known, and this will be an everlasting peace and prosperity.

This encouragement comes from a Source that has never been wrong. To verify this greatest hope that has ever been proclaimed would require volumes much larger than this, many of which have already been written. However, for the sake of this study, we will refer to a few biblical prophecies that shed light on what we are experiencing and what we can do about it.

As we dig down into the truth about Marxism and ourselves, we need to keep this encouragement in mind. The world must experience the ultimate time of darkness before it will wake up to the light and learn what has led us to such human depravity as Marxism. Still, it is difficult to believe human beings could stoop so low to embrace something so evil. Unfortunately, this is the reality we must face before we can be freed from it.

Ultimately, the whole world will wake up to its madness. Marxism is a concoction of the most cruel and evil ways of men, combined with the worst arrogance and pride of men, to bring about the world's worst "bully spirit" and most dominating power. The only way to deal with a bully is to stand up to one. We are now in a place where we have no choice but to stand.

Still, it's not that we must, we get to. The greatest battles require the greatest warriors, and that is what we must become. It must get dark before we can see the stars. Now we expect to see some of the greatest soul warriors ever to emerge.

The third-rate mind is only happy when it is thinking with the majority. The second-rate mind is only happy when it is thinking with the minority. The first-rate mind is only happy when it is thinking.

– A.A. Milne

Chapter 2

Marxist Roots

Darkness Before the Dawn

To distinguish between a democratic, republican form of government and Marxism, it helps to understand the roots of each. Since Karl Marx contended that the American Republic was the arch enemy of Marxism, we will briefly examine our Judeo-Christian roots, including the biblical prophecies our American Republic was founded on. Then we will compare these to the roots of Marxism. As we understand these roots, we will begin to understand the conflict of our times.

Just as the darkest time comes just before dawn, biblical prophecy declares the end of this age will be the greatest time of trouble the world has ever experienced, followed by the greatest time of light, truth, and peace. The troubles are the result of mankind thinking we can run the world without God. Our rulers seek to sever all connections to God (see Psalm 2). In biblical prophecy, the troubles increase until God must intervene to end the madness before mankind destroys all life on earth. But He does more than just save us from darkness and troubles, He restores the earth to the paradise it was originally created to be.

Of course, with our nuclear arsenals, mankind now has the power to obliterate all life on earth. Some who have been at the top of our Department of Defense and other government agencies have said the danger of nuclear war is now more probable than any time during the Cold War. Unfortunately, with this increasing power to destroy our planet, there is no evidence that wisdom has increased, just the opposite. As human philosophy has degenerated into deep darkness, human governments are descending into a terrible pride that will result in ultimate madness.

According to biblical prophecy, after God intervenes to keep men from destroying the earth, His relationship with man will be restored. This will result in the dawning of a new day and the greatest time of peace and prosperity. Not only will there be peace among men but also between men and creation. The earth itself will be fully restored to paradise (see Isaiah 11).

Scripture vividly defines this darkness that will come upon the world at the end of this age. Nothing in history comes as close to fulfilling this as Marxism. According to Scripture, this anti-God/antichrist power will seek to bring the entire world into subjection and will come close to accomplishing this for a short time, then God will intervene.

In biblical prophecy, the only power that seeks to bring the whole world under its subjection is evil, empowered by the evil one. It is the source of the "deep darkness" that covers the world at the end of this age. In Revelation, this power is called "the beast." Then, according to Revelation, there is a second beast, which the first one will give its power to. The only other power currently seeking worldwide domination is radical Islam, and many Islamists have been joining with Marxists to subdue the world, perhaps fulfilling this prophecy of the beasts. If this unity of powers with globalist intentions were to accomplish world domination, they would ultimately fight each other. Because, aside from the doctrine "The enemy of my enemy is my friend," they are incompatible.

In Revelation, the whole world will "follow after" this second beast, and they will impose some things on the world, such as "the mark of the beast" (see Revelation 13). However, there are also some indications that not all nations will be subdued by them. Some will remain loyal to God and His Christ. Of course, the ultimate question for America is: Will our nation be one of these?

Since the only one-world government in Scripture is evil and nearly destroys the earth, Christians have always been resistant to any single government ruling the world except the kingdom of God. Marxism is fundamentally based on the entire world being subjected to a single government and exalts this human government to a place above God. According to Marxism, this government will lead humanity to ultimate conformity.

In contrast to this Marxist philosophy of ultimate conformity, the Scriptures declare that God created the nations (plural) and gave them their boundaries (see Acts 17:26). He even promised to curse anyone who moved those boundaries (see Deuteronomy 19:14; Proverbs 22:28). Evidently, God wanted to preserve the uniqueness of the nations and protect their distinctions and heritage.

This allows for a unity of diversity which preserves the uniqueness of every nation and tribe as He created them.

Any human one-world government is built on the belief that man can run the world without God, and herein lies the root of the ultimate clash at the end of this age. Some seek and serve God; others oppose any acknowledgement of or allegiance to God. The world is about to learn the ultimate lesson in what happens when man tries to exclude the Creator from His creation.

Freedom vs. Slavery

Marxism is a composite of the three most deadly and destructive philosophies ever to have infected the world—Darwinism, Freudian psychology, and Marx's demented philosophy of government and economics. How these combined to bring the most evil and deadly movement the world has ever known is a study in how the worst characteristics of fallen man came to maturity and fed each other. All three seek to rid mankind of belief or allegiance to God and replace it with twisted beliefs of what mankind should be. Marx's declaration to "dethrone God" sounds like the biblical declarations attributed to Satan.

As we dig deeper into the roots of Marxism, we must also dig deeper into what history reveals about human nature to understand the increasing dangers of human arrogance—the root of virtually every human crisis. The Founders of the American Republic saw this flaw in human nature and sought to establish a government to help restrain it, while facilitating the initiative and creativity of people. This was unique in history. It has not worked perfectly, but it has worked better than any other human system of government.

Instead of providing restraints upon flawed and selfish ambition, Marx devised a government and economy that would restrain freedom and inhibit and punish initiative and creativity, while giving government seemingly limitless power to oppress and dominate people. Claiming to liberate mankind, Marxism is an even more cruel bondage than feudalism was in the Middle Ages.

Marxism is built on the most extreme and cruel aspects of what could be the ultimate bully spirit. It is the ultimate slave-master that rules by domination and intimidation using the cruelest forms of mental and physical torture on its subjects. Marxism is the world's ultimate form of slavery for all except the tiniest elite that make up the Marxist state.

In contrast, democratic republics were devised to fundamentally restrain power and its potential abuse of its citizens. A true republic is devoted to the rights of its people and the protection of them against any form of tyranny or oppression.

The Marxist philosophy of man is the opposite of what God created man to be. In Scripture, man was made in God's image. This means more than having a body that looks like His. It means man was given a part of God's creative nature that was not given to any other creature. Democratic republics were devised to help facilitate such creativity which requires liberty.

God so loves to create; He made every snowflake different and every tree and person unique. God also loves unity but His is a unity of diversity, not of conformity. The highest kind of unity is one in which everyone learns to respect the uniqueness of others, learns from one another, and appreciates and honors those who are different without fear or arrogance.

When the Scripture says, **"God made man in His image" (see Genesis 9:6)** it means God made all of mankind in His image. The image of God is so great and diverse that no one group or tribe could contain His image. It takes all of mankind together to do this. In Scripture, the only race that is recognized is the human race. All others are called "tribes" or "nations." Just as Israel was comprised of twelve tribes but one nation, so mankind is made up of many tribes but one race.

Pride and fear are ultimate evils that seek to control men and cause harmful and deadly divisions among people groups. In Scripture, we are repeatedly told **"God resists the proud, but gives grace to the humble" (see James 4:6; I Peter 5:5).** We are also told that pride comes before a fall (see Proverbs 16:18). Pride came before the first fall, and it has led to nearly every fall since. If we walk in arrogance considering ourselves superior to others, this will create harmful, dangerous divisions. If we walk in fear of those who are different from us, it will do the same. Thus, racism or basing our identity on superficial distinctions such as skin color is an ultimate evil and contrary to the nature God gave us.

Marxism's remedy for the destructive divisions a forced unity of mankind creates is to have one powerful, dictatorial government under which all must conform. The purpose of this is to compel everyone to be and think the same about everything. Such unity of conformity can only be achieved by severe punishment, including death to anyone who displays nonconforming thoughts or behavior.

Unity by compulsion is nothing more than false, superficial unity. You can train a parrot to say and do what you want, but it does not come from its heart. You can put people in jail to make them behave as you want, but when you let them out what is in their heart will quickly manifest. We saw this demonstrated by the multitudes who fled to freedom when the Iron Curtain collapsed.

This humanly contrived unity is what Karl Marx envisioned for people. To know what Marx really thought, we need to examine the man himself. Marx was such a demented and cruel person that virtually all who knew him considered him the most despicable person they had ever met. In a remarkable way, Marxism mirrors the nature of Marx in that it also manifests the most despicable, cruel, evil, and twisted aspects of man.

In contrast to this ultimate evil government of Marxism, the American Republic was built on respect for and the protection of individuals to pursue happiness and fulfillment as they see fit. The government exists to protect the rights of individuals to be unique and have unique pursuits, so long as they do not violate the rights of others or bring harm to the community. This freedom released an initiative in people never before seen. It also created a greater advancement in civilization in two hundred years than had been experienced in the previous six thousand years.

Why We Are Enemies

Marx and Marxists rightly saw America as the arch enemy of their demented concept of mankind's future. Marx believed individuals had no value or special rights other than to serve the state. He even referred to the state as "the people" to make it sound like everything they do is for the people. This is yet another Marxist deception that is opposite of actual practice. The Marxist state cares nothing about "the people" except for how they can serve the state and the elites that are in power.

In Marxism, what the state thinks is best for the people is absolute and not to be challenged. This makes people automatons. Initiative and creativity are viewed as examples of individual thought and therefore as enemies of the state. This basic Marxist intolerance for independent thought is at the root of what is now manifesting in our schools and colleges, which have been subjected to Marxist indoctrination now for decades.

Man was created to be free, creative, and to have a special relationship with God as we share this creative aspect of His nature. In the biblical narrative, God gave man the special position of cultivating His Garden. He made man to contribute to His creation. God walked with man every day and conversed about it. He intended for Adam to complete the Paradise He had made for man. God wanted man to have an invested part in His creation.

Also in the biblical narrative, the devil rebelled against God and sought to corrupt His highest creation, man. Satan sought to mar the image of God which man bore thereby severing this special connection to God. No other religion or philosophy on earth so accomplishes this intent to deface and destroy the creative nature of man than Marxism.

Creativity and Freedom

Creativity is born out of freedom. God placed the Tree of the Knowledge of Good and Evil in the Garden and told the first man he could eat from any tree except that one. God did not do this to trap Adam and Eve but to give them the freedom to truly obey or disobey. There can be no true relationship with God without the freedom to reject it. This tree was placed there so they could obey and honor God freely. Freedom requires choice, even the choice not to, which America's Founders also recognized. "Freedom of religion" includes the freedom not to have religion. This remains the cornerstone of all our freedoms.

Again, in the biblical narrative, the first man, Adam, lived in a perfect world. Yet he chose to disobey God and go his own way. Of course, this gave Satan the opportunity to boast: Even God's crowning creation, mankind, when given the choice will choose to rebel against God. As the biblical narrative relates, man may have rejected God, but God did not reject man. Instead, God implemented a plan by which His relationship with man could be restored. A part of this plan included raising up a people who, even in the greatest times of darkness and opposition, would choose to obey God and desire a relationship with Him. Those who made this choice would help Him restore mankind and the earth in the age to come.

This new day for our world will come after the world learns the ultimate fruit of their rejection of God—ultimate darkness and evil at the end of this age. No philosophy or force for evil has come from the darkness of man's fallen heart like Marxism. Marxism is profoundly anti-god and anti-man in its attempt to alter the true nature of man to be a free and creative soul.

The First Republic

This is not meant to be a study in eschatology, biblical prophecy, or end times. However, we must understand the basic Judeo-Christian beliefs of America's Founders and other subsequent democratic republics. The American Republic was the first modern republic and remains the most successful. All recent subsequent republics are unique, which is another fruit of the kind of free-thinking this type of government was intended to release. Still, many republics have adopted many of the same foundations the American Republic is built on.

Long before the American or Greek and Roman republics was the world's first republican government God established for Israel in the wilderness. Moses was sent by God to set His people free, so they could connect to God as their King. God had Israel choose seventy elders among the thousands of elders in Israel. These seventy were to be ruling elders. Since the people chose these governing elders, this was the first known republican form of government. However, this was not to be a substitute for God's leadership but to facilitate it and allow the people to have input. We can see by this how much Almighty God values people's freedom.

In the next couple of chapters, we will continue to dig down into the roots of Marxism and contrast that with democratic republics, its ultimate antithesis in government. In doing so, we will begin to understand the human conflicts of our time as well as what must be done to thwart this ultimate attempt to enslave all mankind.

The teachings of the Bible are so interwoven and entwined with our whole civil and social life that it would be literally—and I do not mean figuratively, I mean literally—impossible for us to figure to ourselves what that life would be if these teachings were removed. We would lose almost all the standards by which we now judge both public and private morals— all the standards toward which we, with more or less resolution, strive to raise ourselves. Almost every man who has this life-work added to the sum of human achievement of which the race is proud—of which our people are proud—almost every such man has based his life-work largely upon the teachings of the Bible.

– **President Teddy Roosevelt**

Chapter 3

Marxist Roots: Part 2

The Road to Hell

As the saying goes, "the road to hell is paved with good intentions." This is not a baseless statement but has been proven many times over. Some of the most destructive, evil forces the world has ever known began with good intentions. Understanding why may help explain how much of the world has been seduced by Marxism, and perhaps save some who still breathe free from the same fate.

Though Marx himself may have formulated his doctrine with the vilest, evil intentions, many Marxists begin with good intentions. They sincerely want to be a part of what they think will be good for all mankind. However, the good side of the Tree of the Knowledge of Good and Evil is just as deadly as the evil side. The humanistic good that Marxism promotes has invariably turned into a terrible, deadly evil—the opposite of what Marxism promises. Though this has been repeated in every nation where Marxism has gained control, people continue to eat from that deadly tree.

Perhaps for the same reason the original Tree of Knowledge was so seductive—its fruit was appealing. The propaganda of Marxism sounds good but it's a deadly poison that nearly always brings death. Unfortunately, few do their "due diligence" to probe beyond the propaganda. Doing wise due diligence about what we believe is not difficult, but it can possibly save our lives. So, let's address some basic principles of due diligence.

Unmasking Evil

As stated, the world's continued tolerance and acceptance of Marxism despite its track record is one of the greatest enigmas of all time. How can so many be fooled by something so blatantly evil? Today, we have nearly a century of experience with Marxism, yet Americans and many world leaders still tend to believe Marxist propaganda over clear facts. Instead of waking up to the terrible demonstrations of cruelty and evil that Marxism perpetrates, Western leaders have become increasingly weak, inept, and naïve to them. How?

First, we are prone to elect naïve and inept leaders. Historically, Marxists have been most effective in getting people to believe their words even when their actions prove otherwise. Politicians do the same. They say the way to tell if a politician is lying is if their lips are moving. This has proven true.

Not to imply that there are no honest people holding political office. Politicians can be some of the most honest people if they can maintain integrity in such an environment. Sadly, however, studies reveal that most people make decisions based on emotion rather than reason, and politicians have learned to appeal to those emotions, and it works. The candidate who appeals to the right emotions is more likely to get elected. Those who appeal to reason, not so much.

Winston Churchill said the biggest argument against democracy is a ten-minute conversation with the average voter. Ultimately, if we have bad or dishonest people in government it is because we the people have allowed it. So, the first accusing finger needs to be pointed at ourselves.

As stated, there are a few true and even extraordinary leaders that have been elected, but they are few and getting fewer. True leaders want nothing to do with the corrupt two-party system we have evolved into. Our first President, George Washington, warned that having political parties would lead to this. Our country was not made to be run by politicians but by leaders and statesmen who refuse to play the evil game of politics and seek rather to do what is right for the people. Politicians have since uprooted this original system, allowing emotions to displace reason.

The twentieth century was the most traumatic in history, but did we learn anything from it? As Bill Monroe, the founder of Bluegrass music, once said, "There's no education in the second kick of a mule." How does civilization endure such pain and not learn anything from it? Because too often we focus on getting rid of the pain instead of locating the source of the pain. Marxism is just the mule that has been kicking us over and over, and it will continue to do so until we learn its true nature and avoid it.

John the Baptist said we must stop flailing at the branches and put the ax to the root of the tree (see Luke 3:9) That is what must be done with Marxism. It cannot be tolerated, but the whole tree must be cut down and its roots destroyed, or it will keep coming back until it finally overtakes us. Marxists are bent on destroying us and our individual freedoms. Why do we continue to tolerate such evil, cruelty, and oppression which has clearly stated it intends to destroy us?

The Poison

The saying is true, "Those who do not know history are doomed to repeat it." This has certainly been true for America since we have allowed our history to not only be forgotten but also to be demeaned and distorted to the point that it now feeds the deception of Marxism.

God commanded Israel to recount their history every year at their appointed feasts, so they would not forget it or repeat its lessons. When Israel stopped recounting their history, they fell into ever-increasing debauchery which led to exile and enslavement by other nations. How could any nation that had been given so much understanding and had such a glorious history allow this? How does America allow this now? By not knowing our history and by allowing those who are bent on destroying us to rewrite our history, so that it undermines our greatest strengths to those who now study it.

Not knowing history has allowed much evil to come on the earth and to be repeated. Marxist deceivers know this and have set out to revise our history to deny us the important truths and lessons our history provides. In its place, American history now promotes their agenda and propaganda. Our sleepy school boards allowed Marxist historical revisionists to do this, setting the stage for emerging generations to be immunized against the deadly siren song of Marxist socialism, while simultaneously learning to hate their own heritage.

At this writing, Critical Race Theory (CRT) is becoming a controversial subject. That's a good thing, as it reveals at least some are waking up to what is being done in our schools. To embrace CRT, one would need to be almost completely ignorant of our true history and already embracing the Marxist revisionist version instead. In articles published today, CRT is being compared to Maoist teachings which led to devastation in China, and the death of up to 100 million people in the Chinese Cultural Revolution. It is encouraging to see some parents and journalists beginning to understand the link between Marxism and Critical Race Theory.

Later, as we address the Marxist 45-part plan for destroying America, we will cover more deeply how Marxists use historical, cultural, and social wounds to divide the people and nations they are targeting. Many of their lies have truth attached to them and sometimes many truths, which they use to mask their deadly lies. Much like rat poison is 98% food to mask the 2% poison.

Every nation has social injustices in their history. This can leave social and cultural wounds that may not be healed with the passage of time. Like physical wounds, social wounds need to be opened, cleaned, dressed in antiseptic, and closed properly to heal. Marxist strategy is the opposite—to find unhealed wounds they can agitate and infect to cause division. They are good at this.

We now find ourselves facing a global Marxist tidal wave created by a combination of the brilliance of Marxist deceivers combined with our own leaders' incompetence, ignorance, and naiveté. There are other contributing factors, but these are the main ones. And if not confronted, this will soon lead to increasingly deadly strife and division. This is what Marxists are trained to do—agitate until we succumb to anarchy. Marxists know that once people experience anarchy, they are ready to embrace Marxist totalitarian control to replace it.

Back to the Future

Karl Marx wrote and taught that Western democratic leaders were so naïve they would pay for the Marxist revolutions that would destroy them. This was not only an insult; it has also proven true. Some of America's most wealthy industrialists helped fund the Bolshevik Revolution and have likely contributed to every Marxist revolution since. This is happening now. Major U.S.-based corporations are helping fund a Marxist revolution in America by supporting Marxist-led organizations like Black Lives Matter and Antifa. Though these corporations are certain to be seized by the Marxists immediately if they come to power. Still, we need to know why and how they do this if we are to stop it.

Vladimir Lenin boasted his treatise on Marxism did not contain a single truth, yet it went viral at the time and was embraced by some of the most wealthy and powerful capitalists who were their main targets for destruction. Lenin's treatise was so widely lauded among Western leaders and intelligentsia it became one of the most widely distributed treatises in history. This shocking level of naiveté by many leading Western citizens was proof to the Marxists that Marx was right: the West will ultimately be destroyed by the capitalists who funded it.

Two Witnesses

Not to be confused with the two witnesses in Revelation, the two biggest sagas of our time is *The Lord of the Rings* and *Star Wars*. Both have identical themes that have proven to be prophetic. In them, the whole world, or in the case of Star Wars, the whole galaxy is being controlled by an ultimate evil that is threatening to crush the last remnants of the faithful. The good are so outnumbered it seems they have no chance, yet they refuse to quit. They resolve to die rather than retreat any further before this ultimate evil.

As the last battle rages, a couple of hobbits, or Jedi knights in *Star Wars*, bring down the greatest evil of all time. This is also prophetic. It does not take many to bring down this ultimate evil that is now dominating our world. It only takes a few faithful ones, which means "full of faith," who are committed to never quitting.

We must stand and fight this evil because it is evil, regardless of how impossible our success may seem. Better to die fighting evil than to live under it. We must never give up hope. Our God seems to get involved in our battles only when they become impossible for us. This story has already been written. You can read the end of the Book and know that truth will prevail over every lie and ultimately restore the earth from the damage of this great conflict.

The Plan

As the saying goes, "Any jackass can kick a barn down, but it takes a skillful carpenter to build one." Marxism is a destroyer, not a builder. It has destroyed many nations but has not made one better. Our battle is against this ultimate destroyer that is bent on tearing down every good thing we have built.

Marxists have had as their primary goal the destruction of the American Republic. They view America as the seedbed of liberty which Marxism cannot tolerate. Marx even admitted that Marxism would never work so long as there was a single capitalist economy, because Marxism cannot compete with the productivity of a free market. Everything about Marxism destroys the initiative that free markets are built on, including the free, creative, and innovative people who fuel that advancement.

Instead of seeking to build something better, Marxists simply destroy all their competition until they are the only game left in town. Marxists boast they are the builders of the coming utopia, but their definition of utopia is so ambiguous only the most ignorant and naïve can believe them.

Many can be ignorant or naïve when made to believe they are brilliant for siding with Marxism. Marxists tend to think they know more than others and to know more than they do. But that is their weakness and why they become reactionary when challenged to defend their shallow principles.

The generations that experienced or witnessed the horrors of Marxism will not be easily fooled again. More recent generations, who have not witnessed the butchery, cruelty, and impoverishing of so many nations remain as naïve as former generations at their age. So, a primary target of Marxism remains youth, whom they consider easily blinded by idealism and the delusion they also know more than they do.

Let's face it, we were all young once. I was a Marxist until I read Karl Marx's works. Then I realized, I was just a rebel who had gravitated to Marxism because it fed my rebellious nature. Except for the ambiguous claim to build a utopia for man, Marxism is all about tearing down and destroying with little concept of building anything. Its only vision is platitudes and destruction.

Marxists are brilliant, strategic, and effective destroyers. They get to know their enemies better than their enemies know themselves. They see their weaknesses and devise workable plans for exploiting them. To destroy America, Marxists boast that they will use our own Constitution and Bill of Rights to destroy the foundations of our Republic. They are brilliant at this.

Marxists are open about how they will use our courts and our courts have proven easy prey for their diabolical schemes. Our own government shields Marxists while they are busy destroying us. In a way, Marxists have become as confident as the 1960's Green Bay Packers football team. They were so dominant when they lined up to play, they would tell the opposing team what play they were going to run, then dare them to stop them. They were hardly ever stopped. Marxists have been doing the same to America— publicly boasting about their strategy to destroy us, while our leaders let them do it!

As Marxists have worked hard to sow the seeds of division in our people that would seal our doom, our leaders have repeatedly defended and even aided them. We believe politicians who lie to us every time they talk. How long will we allow this?

The next step in the Marxist plan to destroy America is to foment another American civil war. During or after that, the plan is to create anarchy, knowing that anyone who experiences the horrors of anarchy will gladly submit to totalitarian Marxist rule. This same strategy has worked in dozens of countries and has rarely failed. Still, it has been stopped when exceptional and competent leadership arose to oppose it.

One would think with so much evidence of Marxist strategy and how they have implemented it, American leaders would know and counter this. Instead, with few exceptions, our American leaders have proven to be the most naïve, inept, and easiest pushovers yet. We don't just need new leaders; we need a new breed of leaders who are not politicians.

At this writing, there are Bills in the U.S. Congress that, if passed, will be the final nails in the coffin to the freedoms our American Republic was built on. It may take time for their impact to play out, but the last remaining moorings to our Constitution and Bill of Rights could be severed by these laws. Then the door will be completely open for Marxists to use our own federal government as the primary vehicle for their subjugation of America. This is happening at lightning speed. And presently, it seems the remaining champions of liberty and our Republic don't even know what hit them.

Still there remains hope. It is not too late to preserve our Republic and freedom, but we have no time to waste. We must recover the strong foundations our country was built on and wake up to the deceptive traps this most deadly enemy of Marxism has set for us.

The Trumpet Sounds

Nations much smaller, weaker, less-advanced, and less-sophisticated than America have woken up and thwarted Marxist agendas in the past, just before they succeeded. Here was their simple strategy:

1. Wake up! Sound the alarm about what is happening.

2. Stand with courage and resolve to never surrender to this evil, knowing it only takes a few to turn the tide.

3. Settle for nothing less than total victory, eradicating the Marxist lies from every place they have been sown into the fabric of our country, especially recovering education and the media until they become fortresses of truth instead of lies.

This strategy is simple but not easy. We must resolve to pay any price and never surrender to this insidious evil. It will require the same willingness to fight and sacrifice to save our country as it did to found it. This is our time. We must not allow what so many paid so much to found and preserve be lost on our watch.

There is more to understand about the roots of Marxism. We will cover these as we examine their counterpoints found in our Republic, Constitution, and Bill of Rights—the most powerful government documents ever written. Unfortunately, even with the best form of government, we are only as good as our people. Leadership is the main issue. Recognizing both pseudo and real leaders must be a part of this study as well.

Some problems will only yield to daring, bold and decisive actions. When the situation warrants it, be aggressive, take audacious action.

– R. Redwine

Chapter 4

The Spirit of Marxism

Part 1

Even a cursory study on Marxism should reveal there are spiritual powers behind trends, movements, and world events. In the same uncanny way, the character and nature of every Marxist movement has taken on the nature and character of Karl Marx. So, to understand Marxism and to know the degree of influence it can have on a person, organization, or agenda, we need to understand Marx.

Intolerance

As mentioned, Karl Marx was described by those who knew him as the most despicable person they had ever met. If anyone questioned one of his principles or theories, Marx would not only reject them; he would also scorch the earth to destroy them. This has characterized every Marxist movement or government since. In fact, the more intolerant they are of any kind of challenge or debate, the greater the Marxist influence.

We now see this inability to accept challenges or differences of opinion in our schools and universities. At first, such ideas or challenges are met with scorn, shunning, or retribution in the form of bad grades. Then, as Marxist influence grows, the intolerance grows into accusations, threats, and even violence.

This trend is now obvious in our schools, but also in the media, social media, and arts and entertainment. At first, actors and actresses who dared reveal a contrary opinion to the leftist agenda were ridiculed. Now they are banned from Hollywood. Such intolerance is contrary to the freedoms America was founded on and has exacerbated the growing divisions in our country. In fact, this inability to accept debate, challenges, or other opinions is unamerican. The freedom to disagree and openly debate has been a basic part of American culture from its inception and is a major reason for our great advances in nearly every field. It is a fundamental characteristic of freedom.

In every country where Marxists have taken over, any deviation from the party line or policy brings swift punishment. This punishment can be anything from execution to banishment in labor camps where death may be slower but far more painful. At this writing, Marxists do not yet have the power to take such extreme measures in America, but we are quickly moving in that direction. As Marxist influence has grown in the cultural power centers of America, banishment from professions and character assassinations are now almost certain for anyone who does not bow to the Marxist agenda.

This "bully spirit" inability to tolerate a challenge or question is part of the basic nature and core of Marxism. Most of us have either encountered or witnessed a bully. They seek to threaten and intimidate people into submission. The more one surrenders to their intimidation, the more demanding and dominating the bully becomes. This pattern can be found in every Marxist assault on a nation or culture.

But when you finally stand up to a bully spirit you usually find that bully to be a coward. The basic nature of Marxism is to prey on the weak and wounded but then to back down or flee when confronted by a serious challenge.

We see these same characteristics in Climate Change agendas. Real scientists expect and appreciate challenges to their hypotheses, while the overreaction of Climate Change scientists to challenges is not only contrary to the nature of science but is also the nature of Marxism. Today, if you are just skeptical of Climate Change you can lose your job or even be banned from the field of science. Universities can lose grants and companies can lose government contracts just for employing a Climate Change skeptic.

Such totalitarian thinking is contrary to and does great damage to true science.

Such maddeningly inconsistencies were manifested in the attempts to manage the recent pandemic. While we are grateful for the progress science has made and the benefits we now enjoy, the growing politicization and Marxist influence on science has the potential to turn this benefit into a dangerous tool of tyranny.

Dysfunction

Karl Marx was profoundly dysfunctional. His family suffered poverty to the point of starvation, yet he refused to work and provide for them. He believed it was their privilege to suffer for him, so he could spend his time studying at the library. He believed civilization should accept all his proposals without question, and his rage was boundless toward anyone who challenged or refused to recognize his genius. He was in a constant state of rage against everyone and everything. Some of his children chose suicide over living in the dark, angry world he created for them. That is life under Marxism—darkness, depression, and humiliation under a constant threatening authority whose expectations no one can measure up to.

To the degree that Western democratic governments have submitted to Marxist/socialist principles, they, too, have become dysfunctional and incompetent. Every day we see how far we have fallen from good management in government. Most real leaders and good managers will have nothing to do with our government, now that it is in such a state of disrepair.

Marxist governments are built on totalitarian domination far more than effective management principles. They promote political compliance rather than competence. Decisions are based entirely on political agendas over what works. Such increasing incompetence and inefficiency are the basic nature of every Marxist government.

Intimidation

One example of how far Marxism has penetrated our federal government was when President Trump was elected. The Left immediately sought to discredit the election and legitimize his presidency. They called it their "patriotic duty." They never produced a shred of evidence of election fraud, nor of the Russian collusion they invented, while continuing to hammer their narrative of illegitimacy. When President Biden took office, to even question the legitimacy of his election was called "treason."

There is a mountain of evidence that the 2020 election was subject to the worst voter fraud in American history. The diminished value and integrity of the vote threatens the very core of our democratic republic. Those who resist examining voter fraud are in fact the ones committing treason. Such overreaction by the Left when an election is being challenged is a clear sign that something very dark is being hidden. Marxism survives the same way Karl Marx hid the insanity of his ideas by attacking anyone who questioned them with vicious threats until they backed down. We can never back down from Marxism if we are to save our country.

A popular definition of a "racist" today is anyone who starts winning an argument against a liberal. In the arena of serious debate and ideas, Marxists don't have a chance, so they resort to name-calling and destroying people's reputations to avoid being questioned, just as Karl Marx did. Presently, if you have not been called a "racist" or worse, you are not yet in the fight against this oppression that now threatens to overtake us. Such an accusation is and should be a badge of honor for those engaged in this ultimate battle for liberty.

Today, true scientists must have uncommon courage to stand up to this bully spirit. If science does not remain aloof from politics, true science will perish. This courage is noticeably absent within our governmental, bureaucratic scientists who are now lauded as "experts." These so-called "experts" in nearly every field of science now hold these positions for political compliance rather than scientific competence. That is basic Marxist strategy, and it is devastating to science, which the modern world has come to rely on.

This is not to imply that compromised scientists are Marxists. They may be conservative or nonpolitical. However, if they have caved to the pressure to conform, they fall into the category of what Marxists call "useful idiots." Again, to allow political considerations to color scientific findings is contrary to science, but then Marxism makes everything political. The result is what we have now—a lot of fake news and fake science. There are courageous holdouts, but they are increasingly few and embattled.

Marxists are brilliant at spinning everything to fit their political agendas. The Covid-19 pandemic was real and serious, but the way it was handled by our government had all the signs of being used as a political agenda to condition people to submit to government policy. That is also a basic Marxist strategy, as we will soon see when we cover the Marxist 45-part plan for destroying America.

We need good government and should be thankful and supportive of it when we have it. However, no earthly government has earned the right to total blind submission. The way our American government was designed, the government works for the people, not the other way around. The people are responsible for overseeing and challenging everything the government does. Of course, we should do this respectfully, but it is both basically and uncompromisingly American to question government policy to ensure our policies are wise, just, and right.

Preying on the Weak and Wounded

As mentioned, Marxist operatives are taught to discern and attack weakness. They are also taught to recruit the weak and wounded. They know weak and wounded people are easily manipulated and tend to be submissive soldiers of their cause. Wounded people are easily embittered and easy to incite to rebellion and even violence when necessary.

Jesus called Satan "Beelzebub," which means, "lord of the flies." Witnesses to great battles have recounted the sound of many flies swarming to the battlefield as a loud roar. This is because flies swarm to wounds. Every time a fly lands it defecates and any disease it has picked up is passed on to the wound. This can cause infection which makes it difficult if not impossible for a wound to be healed.

Likewise, Marxists seek wounds and infect them with poison that make them nearly impossible to heal. Unhealed wounds, such as those caused by rejection, have been the source of some of the world's most diabolical doctrines, including Nazism and Marxism. Both Marx and subsequent Marxist leaders taught the exploitation of wounded people as a strategy for sowing seeds of division and bitterness which lead to revolutions.

Today, America is under such a concentrated assault, and the fabric of our union will rip apart if this is not soon recognized and dealt with. The way to heal an infected wound is to open it, cleanse it, dress it with disinfectant, then close it back properly. Since many unhealed social wounds are now being opened, what the enemy intends for evil can be used for good, if we properly address and heal them. However, the process of healing can be painful and requires more care and attention than we can give in this study. Still, what is meant for evil can be turned around and used for good.

Ultimate Pride

Marx considered himself the ultimate genius. He believed all mankind should conform to his concepts and theories. Those that did not conform should be eradicated for the good of mankind. Marx may have been the person who most conformed to the nature of the biblical Lucifer who likewise seeks to destroy all who will not worship him.

The Bible tells us, pride comes before a fall. In the biblical narrative, it was pride that caused Satan to fall, and pride has remained at the root of nearly every fall since. The ultimate pride of man may be personified in Karl Marx. His folly led to the most miserable lives imaginable for himself and his family. Likewise, for all who are subjected to his philosophy, a life of profound misery and want awaits.

Again, when Marx was challenged, he not only rejected those who challenged him, he would also not rest until he had destroyed them. When local business people called his ideas crazy, he resolved to destroy not only their business but the entire world of business! In his eyes, capitalism was the supreme evil of mankind that needed to be eradicated.

Friedrich Engels is said to be the only person who could get along with Marx because he never questioned anything Marx said and practically worshipped him. He lavished continual high praise on his foolish theories. He also financially supported Marx, so he could spend all his time developing his delusional theories.

Marx was so loathed by those who knew him, only six people came to his funeral, and at least two of them were paid pallbearers. What his theories produced was supposed to result in the "perfect man," the Marxist man, a brutalized automaton stripped of its individuality and humanity and inevitably hated by all.

Colorless

Marx and his family lived drab, dreary lives of extreme poverty, which is exactly what every nation subjected to Marxism becomes. Not only is the Marxist economy counterintuitive to productivity, it also always results in the impoverishing of those subjected to it. It is by necessity a police state. And now with modern technology this policing can be far worse than Nazi Germany's Gestapo.

Since the basic goal of Marxism is unity of conformity no expression of individuality or creativity is tolerated. Even in the most lenient Marxist states, it is nearly impossible to find people who show any color except drab gray or green.

Everyone is afraid to stand out because that would indicate a lack of conformity and make them a target of the state.

Soon after the Iron Curtain collapsed, I took a train across what had been East Germany. It was like being in a black-and-white movie. The lack of color was striking, and the deep depression of the people was still palpable. A little more than a year later, I went into some of those same areas curious of what I might see after they had experienced freedom. The colors were striking! It seemed every window had a flower box with brilliant flowers growing in them. Many houses had been repainted in bright colors. Most of all, the people were amazingly happy!

Pseudo Geniuses

As you may have noticed by now, all these characteristics of Marxism overlap and are interconnected. Another study in Marxist tactics today is how Marx made Engels feel like he was also a genius for recognizing his genius. This is another characteristic of a Marxist state: the compliant ones are considered the most brilliant for recognizing the genius of Marxism. This is how they recognize their "experts." Those who are compliant are called the most brilliant even if they are the most incompetent. In Marxism, all good and evil revolves around political compliance.

Likewise, the noncompliant are considered demented, foolish, and insane. Such were often placed in insane asylums where they were subjected to shock treatments intended to wipe out memory and remove any possible independent thought or action.

Even after treatment, those sentenced to asylums would be marginalized and could not be trusted with responsible jobs or positions. They were also shunned by family and friends who were afraid of receiving the same treatment. Some were kept alive as a warning to the others, but millions were starved and tortured to death under Marxist dictators.

Summary of Part I

As we see how the nature of Marx is reflected in Marxism, we can also see how Marxism is a composite of the worst evils in government ever to have emerged from mankind. This will become even clearer as we continue in Part II.

Part II

The Battle for Life

As mentioned, Karl Marx's family life and virtually every relationship he had except for Engels was bitter and painful. Marx seemed to have hardened himself to not feel any remorse or pity for others. Even when his children committed suicide, he seemed unaffected. Here, we see the foundations for the evil by which Marxists justified murdering between one and two hundred million people in the twentieth century, making it the deadliest evil the world had ever experienced.

Healthy relationships and high esteem for others is necessary for healthy human life. The first thing God said was not good was aloneness (see Genesis 2:18). He created mankind for companionship. Being alone is a terrible experience for anyone, which can lead to increasingly unhinged behavior. In fact, those who commit the worst crimes, such as mass murderers are often found to be loners. And since no one except Engels could stand to be around Marx, he was no doubt a lonely person, which likely helped fuel his bitterness and contempt toward people, the world, and human life in general.

One of Marx's main goals for forming the perfect state was to destroy the traditional nuclear family. He considered families the primary rival to state allegiance. Thus, Marxist governments implement the most diabolical policies to destroy families and all other human relationships.

One primary Marxist strategy for destroying relationships is to promote and give the highest awards to anyone who turns in others for criticizing the state, its policies, or for exhibiting independent thought. Children that turn in their parents or parents that turn in their children receive the highest honors. Since all relationships are built on trust, this intentional breaking down of that trust is very effective in unraveling and destroying families and relationships in Marxist societies.

Likewise, anyone reporting a neighbor or coworker for independent thought, or for criticizing the state or its policies is rewarded and often promoted. Those turned in can be convicted by even one uncorroborated witness. They can be publicly sentenced to prison, labor camp, or execution. Clearly, this sows distrust in everyone. In my interviews with those who had lived in Marxist states, I learned that everyone had to live with the deception of constantly trying to demonstrate their love and allegiance for a state they hated. This created such a deep conflict in their life that it sapped all their joy and happiness.

Recent studies have found that human relationships are the basis for human happiness. Good relationships effect happiness more than wealth, possessions, or accomplishments. That is why depression in Marxist societies is so palpable and humor difficult if not nonexistent.

Depravity resulting from the loss of human relationships cannot be filled by love and trust for the state, as Marx thought. The opposite happens—an increasing hate and distrust for the state by the people. As studies of human happiness have found, nothing can fill the void of losing trust and relationships with family, friends, neighbors, or coworkers. As the world witnessed the fall of the Iron Curtain and the suppressed rage of the people was released, Marxist government officials had to flee for their lives. Many of them did not make it.

Life and Creativity

According to Genesis, one of the four main reasons God created man was to cultivate the Garden. Man was created to accomplish something. Psychological studies have shown that people will go insane when deprived of meaningful labor. That is why the resulting unemployment of economic downturns always sees a corresponding uptick in violent crime. Marx's insanity may have been the result of his refusal to do meaningful labor since he considered himself superior to those that did.

Contrary to Marxist propaganda, Marx had a great disdain for common people, as does every true Marxist no matter how much they claim the opposite. Just as Marx was outraged at the world for not recognizing and supporting his genius, the Marxist state does the same. To Marxists, people exist only for their labor that supports the communist party members, so they can live in luxury while the rest of the people grovel in poverty, as Marx's family did.

Marx considered himself such a supreme genius he refused to even consider input from others on matters of social, political, or economic theory. He also had no regard for creative or independent thinking, considering it foolish and wasteful of his time. To him, only the elite such as himself and those who recognized Marxism as the supreme human society were capable of creativity or innovation.

Likewise, any form of creativity or individualism in workers is ruthlessly punished under Marxism. People exist for the state and have no value other than slave labor. Only loyal party members can live in luxury and abundance as provided by the slavery of all others.

Idealism vs. Realism

Human idealism, or the ability to have a better idea for a better world is one of the great drivers of human advancement when coupled with wisdom and initiative. However, the more self-centered and ambitious the idealism, the viler and more destructive it becomes.

Marxist idealism teaches that everyone should do their best and work their hardest for the sake of "the people," which means the state. This may sound noble, but it has never worked. Under Marxism, human relationships are so undermined and destroyed that people fear and distrust one another. So, they are not prone to do more for the sake of others. Under Marxist tyranny, creativity and productivity plummet because one of the main factors in human initiative is destroyed—creating and producing for loved ones.

Ironically, Jamestown, the first English colony in North America, began under a form of communism based on the first-century Jerusalem church model of having "all things in common" (see Acts 2:44). The colony had a common garden everyone was supposed to work in and eat from. But hardly anyone worked because they received the same whether they worked or not. Nearly half the colonists died of starvation within the first two years.

The third year, each colonist was given their own plot of land to cultivate and eat from and no one died of starvation. The next year, they had a surplus which they used to trade with the Indians. After only three years with a basic free-market economy, the colonists reaped such a surplus, they started exporting back to Europe. They became wealthy and able to expand and buy more land from the Indians and started importing better tools and resources to work the land. This quickly strengthened and prospered the colonists even more than if they had found the gold they came looking for. The personal industry and initiative they discovered in themselves brought a much greater return than gold.

When everyone receives the same wage regardless of work, productivity plummets and personal initiative is destroyed. It may sound ideal for everyone to work harder for the common good but only a tiny percentage of people will do this. And even those will not work for long, once they see others doing nothing for the same wage.

The Bottom Line

Politics and economics based on human idealism may sound good, but they never work. Productive and invigorating societies that are advancing and prospering are based on realities, not ideals.

Other factors of Marxism that reveal its presence in a group or agenda will be unpacked later in the Marxist 45-part plan for destroying the American Republic.

History does not long entrust the care of freedom to the weak or timid.

– Dwight D. Eisenhower

Chapter 5

Distinctions Between Marxism & Democratic Republics

Karl Marx identified America as the chief enemy of Marxism. He believed socialism could not prevail until America and all Western style republics were eradicated. At the time, America was by no means the most powerful nation. Yet Marx especially focused on the American Republic because he perceived it to be the source of increasing human freedom and an increasingly powerful free-market economy, which Marxism could not compete with. He was right about this.

The American Republic is not the source of all freedom or free markets, but it was rightly perceived by Marx as the emerging leader of these. It became the strongest counterpoint to Marxism, and thus it remains Marxism's biggest target for destruction.

To understand why America would be such a huge prize for them, let's examine the distinctions between Marxism and the American Republic and why there will always be a life-and-death struggle between them until one is destroyed.

DISTINCTION #1: Under Marxism, people exist for the state and are the property of the state.

In the American Republic, the state belongs to the people.

Under Marxism, everyone and everything belongs to the state and is allotted and used as the state dictates. In the American Republic, the state exists for the people and the government's basic mandate is to defend the rights and property of the people.

DISTINCTION #2: Under pure Marxism, "personal" or "private" does not exist. All major decisions affecting the people are made by the authorities.

In America, all personal and private affairs are none of the state's business, so long as no laws are violated. Individuals make all personal and private decisions for themselves.

Under Marxism, the state makes every major decision for the people, including where they live, where they go to school, where they work, and what they do. Even getting married or having children may require permission from the state. For example, until recently, Communist China would only allow one child per couple and still control the number of children they can have.

In America, all personal and family matters are decided by individuals and there no requirements to notify the state of such decisions.

DISTINCTION #3: Under Marxism, everything that is produced by the people belongs to the state.

In the American Republic, what is produced by people belongs to the people who produced it. The state is charged with protecting the rights of the people to own and use their own creations, as they determine.

Under Marxism, anything an individual creates or develops belongs to the state. Those who build or create may not even be acknowledged or compensated for their work.

In America, the state is required to protect the creative property rights of its citizens. This distinction is why there has been a continual conflict between China and the free world over Creative Property Rights. This concept is fundamentally contrary to Marxism, where all things and all people belong to the state.

A few decades ago, China relaxed some of their policies to allow some personal property and free enterprise. The result was more people were delivered from poverty in a short amount of time than any other time in history. Unfortunately, the Chinese Communist Party retains the right and power to seize any personal property or business it believes to be in its interests, which has happened increasingly in recent times.

A basic law of nature is that most creatures are territorial. What they claim as their territory, they will protect. One can drive down a street and easily detect which homes are owner-occupied and which are rented because personal property typically leads to better management and maintenance. This is yet another reason Marxist economies can never compete with free market economies.

DISTINCTION #4: Under Marxism, policies and laws are dictated by the whims of those who are in power, which can be changed at any time for any reason.

The Constitution of the American Republic sets clear and specific processes for establishing laws. These require much debate and analysis to ensure wisdom and justice in the development of laws and their application.

Life under Marxism is like trying to play a game while the rules are constantly changing, and the referees don't even tell you they've changed until you're penalized. This creates perpetual indecisiveness which further thwarts productivity and economic advancement.

Under Marxism, such changes are often done deliberately to keep people under the control of the state. Unfortunately, this also keeps people in a constant state of confusion and uncertainty regarding expectations.

In contrast, the American Constitution was designed to limit the power of the state and require implemented laws to be carefully processed and crafted for the least possible disruption of the people. When changes become necessary, they are implemented in a way that allows plenty of time to plan for those changes.

DISTINCTION #5: Under Marxism, the state is considered the highest source of law and truth, which is to be obeyed and complied with without question or challenge.

The Framers of the American Constitution held to the belief there was a higher Authority and Law than human government. The purpose of human government was to base its laws on "natural law," or what is clearly seen as "self-evident" in nature.

Because the Marxist state is to be the people's god and highest authority, its dictates and whims are considered immutable and unquestionable. In contrast to this demented philosophy that men are capable of totalitarian rule, the Framers of the American Constitution believed that all men were fallible and corruptible, especially by power. So, they devised a form of government to restrain such evil tendencies in men and governments.

As stated, the Framers of the American Constitution derived some of their basic beliefs about government and law from what they called "natural law," which were laws seen in nature that reflected nature's God. Such laws were considered "self-evident" to anyone willing to look at nature to see how creation reflects the nature of a Creator.

One basic and obvious characteristic of nature is diversity which forms one symbiotic whole. The laws that govern nature are consistent and interconnected. Radical or abrupt changes are rare. Even weather and climate changes tend to be regular and predictable. There may be unpredictable and disruptive changes from storms, earthquakes, and other natural disasters but the normal and regular pattern of life makes adjusting to these changes much easier.

Likewise, there can be unpredictable social upheavals such as wars and natural disasters but having a stable and predictable government can make it much easier to react and cope with these. Such stability in government with major changes coming through a tedious but necessary process would ensure that no radical or whimsical changes would be imposed on the people. This would give people a stability in their government, so they could better navigate their personal lives with confidence.

Of course, the chaos and dysfunction in our current federal government is anything but consistent and stable. That is due mostly to the increasing Marxist totalitarian control that has infiltrated our government. It is forcing policies on us with complete disregard for due process as established by our Constitution.

DISTINCTION #6: The ultimate goal of Marxism is to impose a unity of conformity on people, so all will act and think according to the Marxist worldview.

The American Republic was based on a unity of diversity that respects the uniqueness of individuals, states, religions, and philosophies, all of which are protected so long as they comply with the Constitution.

Again, God's unity and the unity found in creation is a unity of diversity. Therefore, the individual right and freedom to express our uniqueness is a core value of our American Republic. This respect for uniqueness and diversity releases a level of creativity and innovation in America which historians have called the greatest advancement in civilization. America did more in its first two hundred years than had been achieved in the previous six thousand years of recorded history.

In contrast, Marxism imposes a unity of conformity where individual expression becomes a threat to the state, which can bring swift and severe punishment and, of course, silence all creativity and innovation. In fact, virtually every modern advancement in Marxist dominated countries was either stolen or copied from the West.

DISTINCTION #7: Under Marxism, the government is the people's god whom they must trust and give allegiance to for all their provisions and needs.

In the American Republic, the government was designed for a strong and resourceful people, not a dependent one. It is to be the people's servant, existing to defend them, their rights, and property, not to make them dependent on the government for their provisions.

Marx's primary devotion was to "dethrone God" and make the state the people's god. To supplant God and gain the people's allegiance, he sought to make the state the sole provider of people's needs. Stalin used even necessities like food and water to control the people, at times starving millions only to teach them the absolute power and authority of the state.

Since Marxist economics destroys productivity when Marxists take over a nation the simple providing of basic food and essentials quickly becomes a major challenge. The state as god never works well for the people, so to keep from losing control of the people, increasing totalitarian dominance is required.

Until the 1930s, the American federal government never had a mandate to provide for individual needs. Instead, the American Republic was to ensure a just and "level playing field" for production and commerce and to allow people to provide for themselves with their own initiative and resourcefulness. This worked better than any economy in world history until the crash of 1929. The Left used this crash to begin adopting Marxist principles of government which would give the federal government increasing control over its economy.

A good case has been made by economists that America would not have experienced the Great Depression had government not overplayed its hand after the Market Crash of 29. Instead, the government used the crash to begin a slow but radical change to make people more dependent on government and thereby easier to control. This may produce short-term positive results, but it is not sustainable as every Marxist attempt has proven.

Since this trend began to make people increasingly dependent on government as their source, the American population has gone from being nearly 100% self-sustaining producers to now only 50% producing more than they consume, and this percentage continues to shrink every year. As such, those who produce must produce increasingly more to provide for the nonproducers. There comes a point when this is no longer sustainable, and the deepening depravity begins.

DISTINCTION #8: Marxism is built on government as the source of highest wisdom and expertise.

The American Republic was born with the understanding that government bureaucracies are not where wisdom, understanding, or even good management are likely to be found, the people are. In America, the people are considered sovereign and the highest source of wisdom and understanding the government should look to for wisdom and expertise.

As Marxist principles have crept into our government and culture, the subtle belief that government is the highest source of wisdom and expertise has grown in Americans. At the same time, our government has become increasingly incompetent at managing even its most basic responsibilities. Decades-old studies on the efficiency of American bureaucracies revealed that only about 10% of resources being channeled into bureaucracies were being used to meet existing needs. The rest were being consumed by mismanagement and spending on ineffective or counterproductive programs with large amounts being completely unaccounted for and nearly impossible to trace.

Today, nearly every federal government department or agency would make a great case study in poor management. Of course, there are exceptions. Unfortunately, anyone who is productive, instead of being promoted and celebrated, they are often persecuted for making everyone else look bad. This is an even truer statement today than when President Reagan first said it: "Government is not the solution; it is the problem!"

Government is necessary. However, since the U.S. government exists for and works for the people, it is a scandal that it has fallen to such a state of mismanagement and corruption. The Founders were right to establish a government that understood the need for constant challenge and discipline by a well-educated and engaged population that would not tolerate the ineptness and incompetence that is now the culture and standard of our federal government.

We now have abundant evidence that those in even the highest positions of government may have little practical understanding of what they presume to preside over and thereby can weaken and even destroy it. The Covid-19 pandemic certainly proved that the best experts in any field are rarely found in government.

What's worse is, as more of our population becomes conditioned by Marxist indoctrination, more people believe that just because someone works for the government, they must know what they are doing. However, those who still know how to think and evaluate, must see that in virtually every way our government is the very worst at efficiently managing just about anything.

Again, this is not to imply we do not need government. We need a government that stays in its lane and does not try to do what it cannot or should not do. As the Marxist assault on our freedom of speech increases, the natural and necessary process for our government to reach good conclusions and practically implement them will continue to degrade.

Chapter Summary

These are only some of the basic distinctions between a democratic republic and a Marxist state. Now with the infiltration of Marxist and socialist principles into the American federal government, these distinctions are being blurred and the results will be increasingly catastrophic. As the saying goes, "If you do not change your direction, you will end up where you are headed." This is where we are headed. The question is, can we change our direction?

As We Were, Not as We Now Are

Marxism and the American Republic as they were originally designed are opposites in nearly every way. In the 1930s during the New Deal, our federal government started implementing social programs it had no authority in the Constitution to assume. The Constitution is clear: Whatever authority is not specifically given to the federal government in the Constitution is reserved for the states and for the people. In the 1930s, we began drifting into a socialist style government which has since continued to gain speed and scope.

The Constitution was intended to limit the scope of the federal government and to keep most authority and desired programs in state and local governments. Since they are closer to the needs, they could understand and manage these programs more efficiently. When the federal government assumed these roles, state and local governments abandoned them.

At this writing, there are an estimated seven hundred agencies in our federal government. (We could not find anyone in our federal government who knew exactly how many.) Many agencies have undefined purposes. Many others have purposes which were accomplished long ago and are obsolete. Some exist to counter the work of other agencies.

If there is no provision for an agency to shut down, it continues to operate and consume paid staff and resources. Though no one seems to know what they are doing or why. The American people pay for this. Today, about three million people work for our federal government, which is many times the number needed for the work that is being done.

Though admittedly, Marxist strategists have been brilliant at carrying out their plan to gradually subjugate the American Republic, Marxist economics is contrary to productivity and therefore will always lead to increasing incompetence and inefficiency. The mismanagement and waste of our federal government now consumes a huge number of national resources which require the seizing of an increasing proportion of the people's resources to sustain.

The way to fix this is simple. The Constitution was designed to limit the scope and power of the federal government. This would still be the case had the Constitution been adhered to. Thus, the answer to nearly every crisis America now faces is to recover the Constitution as the "supreme law of the land," as it specifies.

By acknowledging the Constitution as the "supreme law of the land" and adhering to it, by requiring our government to rediscover good management principles in all that it does, by eliminating all agencies and positions that do not have a specific needed purpose, we could balance our national budget without raising taxes. We might even have enough surplus to begin paying down our national debt, which was accrued through decades of mismanagement and failure to comply with our federal government's Constitutional mandate.

Marxism, and its stepchild socialism, violate all the basic laws of economic physics and simply cannot be sustained. As Margaret Thatcher said, "Socialism only works until they run out of other people's money." It can only be sustained by seizing the people's resources, but there comes a time when all this has been seized and there is nothing left to feed the beast. These distinctions between Marxism and the American Republic are only the most basic. Others will be addressed as we cover the Marxist 45-part plan for destroying America.

The fundamental basis of this nation's law was given to Moses on the Mount. The fundamental basis of our Bill of Rights comes from the teachings we get from Exodus and St. Matthew, from Isaiah and St. Paul...

– President Harry Truman

❧ Chapter 6 ❧

The Marxist 45-Part Plan for Destroying America

Since Marxism is now making some of its boldest inroads into America, and since it is close to accomplishing its "45 Goals" for taking over America, it is crucial that we examine each goal to understand how they are undermining our Republic. Understanding these goals is a revelation into the nature of Marxism and key to understanding why Marxism is the deadliest evil mankind has ever been subjected to.

These 45 Goals were published in *The Naked Communist* in 1961, which stated they were gleaned from testimonies before Congress, scholars, and the writings of American Communists. In 1963, these 45 Goals were read into the Congressional Record by Albert S. Herlong, Jr., (D-Florida). The ultimate strategy of this plan was to destroy the Judeo-Christian foundations of the American Republic which our freedoms are built on and thereby destroy our Republic. This list is derived from those published in *The Naked Communist* but paraphrased with more current terminology and updated commentary.

MARXIST GOAL #1: U.S. acceptance of coexistence with communism as the only alternative to nuclear war.

From the 1950s until the collapse of the Soviet Union in 1991, the fear of nuclear war dominated the world. This #1 goal explains how Marxists used this fear to further their control of international affairs. Their goal was achieved when the Nixon Administration's Détente policy was implemented. This relaxed policy opened the door wide for the Soviet Union and Marxist insurgents to continue their expansions while accelerating their determination to destroy America and all other free countries. So long as this policy continued, communism advanced and democratic republics were attacked and overtaken at a rapid pace.

After taking office, President Reagan ordered a competitive analysis of the Détente policy to see how it was working. The study revealed a great advantage had been given to the Communists and a great disadvantage to the free world. Reagan quickly developed a new policy of resistance against Marxist aggression. This new policy was more effective than anyone could have foreseen.

President Reagan and Britain's Prime Minister, Margaret Thatcher, were two strong leaders not easily manipulated by communist threats. Instead, they pushed back hard against them. Europeans, who still had not learned after two world wars that appeasement does not work, were appalled by this new resolve to stand up to the bully, but it worked. Communist expansion slowed, and in less than a decade, the Soviet Union imploded.

Many nations were set free from the communist yoke by this collapse. The Cold War was not won by military battles but by the resolve to stand up to the bully spirit of Marxism and boldly declare it an "evil empire."

MARXIST GOAL #2: Make the U.S. willing to capitulate to communist demands rather than risk atomic war.

Until Ronald Reagan and "Maggie" Thatcher stood up to the Soviet bully, most Western leaders cowered before them, repeatedly capitulating to Soviet demands. Even when they had a great advantage over the Soviets in every way, including military force and nuclear arsenals, still they relented. There was some pushback, such as Kennedy's stand during the Cuban Missile Crisis and Nixon's stand during the Jordanian Crisis. However, even after these incidents proved that communists would retreat before strength, Western leaders continued their nonsensical giving in to communist bullying and demands.

Of course, no one wanted nuclear war, but you can never appease a bully. History teaches that trying to do so inevitably leads to war. British Prime Minister Neville Chamberlain's attempts to appease Hitler was a more recent example. Soviet foreign policy was to bully the world into giving them whatever they wanted. If you give a bully what he wants, he will perceive that as weakness and want more.

The weakness of Western leaders allowed communism to expand until about half the world's population was under their yoke. Winston Churchill had contended that the Cold

War could be won without a single shot being fired simply by standing up to the communists. He was right. Reagan and Thatcher's strong and consistent pushback revealed the weakness of the communist system and it quickly fell apart.

It is basic Marxist doctrine to exploit weakness and avoid confronting strength. Even when the West had overwhelming military and economic strength and could easily have decimated Marxism, the West still had weak, easily intimidated, and easily manipulated leaders who allowed themselves to be pushed around. Marxism likely would not have lasted past the 1950s had it not been for weak, inept Western leadership.

MARXIST GOAL #3: Develop the illusion that total disarmament by the United States would be a demonstration of moral strength.

As unlikely a goal as this might seem, a movement arose in the U.S. to unilaterally disarm to prove its moral superiority. It failed but weakened American resolve enough to hand the Marxists many advantages and victories during the Cold War.

This philosophy of unilateral disarmament by the U.S. was embraced by Paul Warnke who negotiated the SALT II treaty with the Soviets. This treaty caused the U.S. to voluntarily surrender its nuclear advantage and to gradually begin dismantling our entire military. This did not make the world safer as Warnke contended. Instead, the Soviet Union continued to build their military strength until it began to outclass the West. This opened the door for even bolder worldwide Marxist aggression.

SALT II also sent a clear message to Marxist revolutionaries everywhere that, if they kept pressuring America, we would gradually surrender everything including our allies and our own country. This emboldened Marxists even more and eroded the courage of our allies, which led to the precarious situation the world is in today.

MARXIST GOAL #4: Have the U.S. permit free trade between all nations regardless of communist affiliation or whether the items being traded could be used for war.

Marx taught that Western capitalists would fund Marxist revolutions just to make a profit. This proved true. Quite possibly no other country in the world has been more poorly served by its foreign policymakers, treaty and trade negotiators, and many of its business leaders than the United States of America. It seems U.S. strategy was to give the communists everything they wanted and ask for nothing in return.

Marxist socialism might not have survived anywhere had it not been for the one-sided trade deals offered by the U.S. and its allies. So many times, these trade deals propped up failing Marxist economies when they otherwise would have collapsed.

After the collapse of the Soviet Union, and after the capital of communism moved from Moscow to Beijing, it's uncanny how Western businesses poured into China. Now it is our greatest threat to freedom, and on its way toward eclipsing American and Western economic and military strength.

Much of this is due to the brilliance of Chinese Communist leaders to exploit weak American leadership. Perhaps even more so was the brilliance of Chinese leadership to borrow and implement basic free market principles from the West. While America and the West have been incomprehensibly turning away from basic free market principles, which our strength and prosperity was built on.

MARXIST GOAL #5: Have the U.S. extend long-term loans to the Soviet states.

The Soviets broke every treaty they entered with the West. Marx and Lenin had advocated this because they perceived Western leadership to be so weak and inept, they knew they could get away with it and they were right. Their doctrine was to make many treaties with the U.S. because they knew they did not have to abide by them, while America would to their own detriment. China has continued this policy. As the Marxists blatantly reneged on every treaty, loan, and agreement, Western leadership continued to give them more money and make more agreements.

Were our leaders really that naïve, or just cowardly? Were our leaders making one-sided deals with Marxists because they knew our shallow media would not dig down into the details to reveal these terrible sellouts? Did they do it to gain political capital at home by appearing to negotiate with communists to keep us out of military confrontations? Other than outright insanity, there doesn't seem to be any other explanations.

Regardless, it is incomprehensible how we are financing the very aggression that is meant to destroy America and the West and freedom-loving people everywhere.

MARXIST GOAL #6: Persuade America and the West to provide aid to all countries regardless of Marxist affiliation.

This is yet another way Marxists steal from the American people and use our resources to fund our own destruction. Communist China never would have become the threat to the world it is today had we not aided them in this way. The very fact that our leaders and elected officials fell for this remains one of the enigmas of history. What's worse is how this continues today with such a long history of policy failure.

MARXIST GOAL #7: Persuade America to recognize Communist China and grant its admission to the United Nations.

Doing this would require America to deny continued recognition and support for the free Chinese government of Taiwan, one of our most trusted allies. We still did it which further projected American weakness and lack of resolve to our enemies and allies. Almost immediately, the United Nations went from being a freedom-protecting "leader of the free world" to one that consistently acts against the interests of the free world and is now a primary platform for promoting and projecting Marxist globalist initiatives.

As we continue to cover these 45 Communist Goals for taking over America in subsequent chapters, we will see how they have affected our present world and how close the Marxist globalist initiative has come to accomplishing their goal of world domination.

The liberties of our country, the freedom of our civil Constitution, are worth defending at all hazards; and it is our duty to defend them against all attacks.

The problem is not to find the answer; it is to face the answer.

– Terence McKenna

❖ Chapter 7 ❖

Marxist Goals for Destroying America 8 through 18

As we continue the Marxist 45 Goals for destroying America, some may seem irrelevant. However, they were still accomplished in a time and a way that effectively weakened America and the free world and are therefore still important to understand.

Some of these goals seem redundant, but they overlap like links in a chain working together. Some were implemented quickly, others with great patience. What is clear is how brilliant the Marxists are in formulating their plan and how ignorant and inept our leaders are to see and counter it.

MARXIST GOAL #8: Set up East and West Germany as separate states despite Soviet promises in 1955 to settle the German question by free elections under the supervision of the United Nations.

Anyone negotiating with a Marxist must know it is Marxist doctrine to negotiate faithlessly. They will break their agreement whenever it is expedient for them to do so. It is incompetence at best for any negotiator not to know this. President Reagan may have been the first Western leader to know and act on this. In regard to any treaty he signed with the Soviets, he said, "trust but verify." He demanded as a condition for signing any treaty the right to have inspections anytime anywhere and frequently ordered such inspections.

He had a resolve Marxists had not seen before in American or Western leaders. His display of strength alone began to fracture the weak foundations of their fragile state. When held accountable to their agreements, they did not have the economic strength to do so, which ultimately led to their collapse.

MARXIST GOAL #9: Prolong the conferences to ban atomic tests because the U.S. had agreed to suspend its testing so long as negotiations were in progress.

We suspended our nuclear tests so long as the Soviets continued to negotiate, while they just kept right on testing. This enabled them to catch up to the West in nuclear capabilities, putting the whole world on edge of nuclear annihilation for decades. This will forever remain a memorial to the naiveté and stupidity of American leaders and negotiators, until the Reagan Administration.

MARXIST GOAL #10: Allow all Soviet satellite nations individual representation in the United Nations.

Everyone knew the Soviet satellite nations were not independent and would only vote in unison with the Soviet central command that controlled them. Even so, the inept leaders of the free world allowed them to do this, giving the majority vote and control of the United Nations to the Marxists. This thwarted virtually every Western initiative through the U.N., thereafter making this organization little more than a platform for Marxist propaganda and expansion as it remains to this day.

When the Islamic states were allowed membership, though they were in violation of basic human rights requirements for membership, this further tilted U.N. business against the U.S. and the West, as these states have almost always sided with the Marxist states.

This also made the U.N. a platform for Marxists and Islamists to continually attack America and the West while blocking our ability to counter their initiatives. Thus, resources collected from America and other free states as U.N. dues are often used for anti-American and anti-Western purposes.

MARXIST GOAL #11: Promote the United Nations as the only hope for mankind. If its charter is rewritten, demand that it be set up as a one-world government with its own armed forces.

Of course, the Marxists wanted this since they had gained control of the U.N. and could therefore count on it as a tool and weapon for world expansion and for attacking America and the West. Apparently enough reason came on Western leaders to prevent this from happening, yet it remains a Marxist goal to this day.

MARXIST GOAL #12: Resist any laws that outlaw the American Communist Party.

Even with the American Communist Party's seditionist strategy and operations, the Supreme Court ruled that outlawing organizations that advocated subversive actions against the United States violated the First Amendment. Consider the contradiction of the Supreme Court agreeing to outlaw yelling "fire" in a crowded theater as not being protected by the First Amendment, while those bent on destroying America and its way of life are now protected by our own Supreme Court as a First Amendment right.

This is just one of many conflicting, illogical, and dangerous decisions by our Supreme Court which has never been challenged or overturned. The Supreme Court has often assumed authority beyond what the Constitution allows. Its wayward decisions have not only caused some of the biggest divisions in our country today but have also allowed some of the biggest threats to our Republic both foreign and domestic to have free rein against us. America will not last much longer if we do not recover the foundation of our democratic Republic: The Constitution is "the supreme law of the land," not the Supreme Court.

MARXIST GOAL #13: Do away with all loyalty oaths.

The main purpose of this goal was to do away with the oath prescribed in Article 6 of the Constitution that every government employee and elected official must take to defend the Constitution from all enemies foreign and domestic. Of course, they want to do away with this oath since they are the biggest enemy of our Constitution. They know if they can destroy this oath, they can destroy our Republic.

Marxists have studied the strengths and weaknesses of our government and understand them better than most Americans, including our own elected officials and leaders. This is a deadly reality that must change soon if we are to continue to exist. Our weaknesses and vulnerabilities do not come from our Constitution but from our leaders' ignorance of our Constitution. Again, we can have the best form of government and still have the worst government if we elect bad leaders.

MARXIST GOAL #14: Continue giving Marxist governments access to the U.S. Patent Office.

Marxist governments do not want access to our Patent Office to protect patents but to steal them. They immediately began stealing them and continue to do so to this day. This has allowed Marxist states to not only accelerate their high-tech military development but has also likely cost American companies and the American people trillions of dollars in lost revenue for their inventions and work.

MARXIST GOAL #15: Capture one or both main political parties in the U.S.

This is another box the Marxists can check. The Democratic Party has moved so far to the left its agenda is now in lockstep with Marxist goals for subverting America. It is also now the main platform from which the Marxist agenda is being promoted.

That is not to say that everyone in the Democratic Party is a Marxist but there does not seem to be any resistance in the party to the Marxist agenda. If any are not Marxists, they are at least complicit for not standing up to them.

Even some in the Republican Party are by their words and actions more aligned with Marxist doctrine than they are with the principles America was founded on. They may vehemently protest this accusation, but their actions betray them. The Democratic Party can now be accurately called the Anti-Democratic Party or Marxist Party.

The Republican Party is not far behind except for a courageous few who have stood against the Marxist agenda and those that promote it. Still, both parties have been bending strongly to the left, so much that even some of those who now call themselves "conservatives" are far left of where the Democratic Party used to be.

Remember, many Marxist operatives don't even realize they are promoting Marxism or know what Marxism is. This is yet another testimony to how effective Marxists are at keeping even their own people ignorant but compliant.

Not only does today's Democratic Party agenda run parallel with the Marxist agenda for subverting America, but many in that party also now admit to and even boast about being socialists without any protest from the others. As we cover the rest of the 45 Marxist goals for subduing America, we will see just how much both parties are now being used to accomplish this.

As we see our leaders, elected representatives, and government officials being so easily outmaneuvered by our Marxist enemies, we must acknowledge how profoundly flawed and corrupt our two-party system is for appointing leaders. George Washington warned us of what would happen if we allowed political parties. He said we should debate issues as Americans, not as party partisans. This is a subject worth far more coverage than we can give here. Suffice it to say our corrupt party system is a major reason our country is in crisis.

MARXIST GOAL #16: Use the courts to weaken American institutions by claiming their activities violate civil rights.

Of course, one foundation of our Republic is the protection of civil rights for all our citizens. We must never abandon our resolve to see this fully realized. However, Marxists have been effective at promoting their seditionist agenda as a civil right and our courts have consistently sided with them.

Both Marxists and Islamists have stated they will use our courts, laws, and our Constitution to destroy us and they have been brilliant at doing so. Those who have sworn "to defend the Constitution from all enemies foreign and domestic" have been at best asleep on watch or at worst complicit. There are still some legislators, lawyers, and judges that deserve our support for standing courageously against this agenda, but such are becoming increasingly rare.

This fight over whether our courts will continue to be used by this Marxist agenda or defend our Constitution will certainly be a major battleground our future will depend on. Still, history affirms it does not take great numbers to bring about change. Even a tiny minority or the one who demonstrates courage can awaken the rest and prevail over what seems like an inevitable tide. We must never give up!

MARXIST GOAL #17: Take control of schools. Use them to transmit socialism and Marxist propaganda. Soften the curriculum. Get control of teachers' associations (unions). Insert the (Marxist) party line into textbooks.

This is another box the Marxists can check. Our children are no longer being educated but indoctrinated by Marxists. American education was once considered among the best in the world. As teachers' associations grew into unions they began to side more with Marxist agendas. Running parallel to this has been the sharp downturn in the quality of American education. Marxists are bent on destroying American education which has enabled America to become such a powerful military and economic force, thwarting their globalist goals. But more importantly, they want to corrupt and further weaken emerging generations of Americans with immorality and perversion.

Many American schools have already begun replacing courses in math and reading with social training in gender, sex, and race education. Meanwhile, American education has now fallen below some third world countries. In 2003, fifteen-year-old Americans measured in the lower half of all nations in math, reading skills, and science literacy as reported by the National Center for Education Statistics. Since then, it has plummeted even further.

What is the teachers' unions answer to this tragedy that is destroying future generations of Americans? Give the unions more money to support their indoctrination of our students with their radical political agendas. What have our elected officials done? Given them more money to further their radical agendas without requiring them to restore effective education.

We should want the best teachers, schools, resources, and equipment for our kids to prepare them for life in the twenty-first century. Instead, the agendas, propaganda, and moral corruption now being fed to our students is destroying America's future, while the quality of American education remains in a death spiral. To throw more money at what is already seriously awry without requiring the necessary changes only brings about the destruction of our children and nation faster.

There are teachers who are courageously trying to stand against the corruption in the teachers' unions and the radical agenda that has increasingly dominated school curricula. Few of them get much support because anyone who challenges the teachers' unions' agenda will be accused of being antieducation. As our elected officials cower before such threats, our children's education and future are being destroyed.

Education is a primary battlefield on which our future will be determined. We cannot continue to be naïve and blind to what is happening to our children and our nation through the perversion of American education.

MARXIST GOAL #18: Gain control of all student newspapers.

This is yet another box the Marxists can check. However, there have been some student groups who have risen to challenge this with a few brilliant strategies of their own. When one college gave their student newspaper to the student Communist Club, all the conservative and Christian students joined the Communist Club. This gave them the majority, so they voted in Christian and conservative officers and retook control of the student newspaper.

As much as it may seem like the enemies of our country are close to destroying our Republic and our freedoms, it is not too late to reverse the damage that has been done to our country. However, it will take courage and sacrifice. This is beginning to happen as a large percentage of Americans have recently begun to home school, or put their children in private schools that are teaching honorable values rather than succumbing to the moral and political indoctrination now going on in our public schools. It should be the resolve of every parent to make the necessary sacrifices for their children rather than to leave them in an education system that allows them to be sacrificed to foreign gods.

You Americans are so gullible. No, you won't accept communism outright, but we'll keep feeding you small doses of socialism until you'll finally wake up and find you already have communism. We won't have to fight you. We'll so weaken your economy until you'll fall like overripe fruit into our hands.

– Nikita Khrushchev, former Soviet Premier

❖ Chapter 8 ❖

Marxist Goals for Destroying America 19 through 27

MARXIST GOAL #19: Use student riots to foment public protest against programs or organizations that undermine socialism.

Before 1960, this was considered an unattainable goal. By the end of the decade, it had been accomplished. During the Anti-Vietnam War Protests, Marxist operatives infiltrated the peace movement to make it more militant and focused on Marxist goals.

Since this was the height of the hippie movement, most people came to the demonstrations touting "peace and love" which was their dominant sentiment. However, certain elements infiltrated these demonstrations to attack police and military security, destroy property, and create overall mayhem. This strategy has since been upgraded to where many of these operatives are now paid professionals.

If we are to counter this, we must first understand the Marxist agenda is a formidable plan and their operatives are highly trained and effective. Their agents may not even know what Marxism, socialism, or communism is, but they are very effective at what they do and have at different times toppled nearly half the world's governments. Now they intend to bring down America.

It may seem like we are suddenly being overpowered by a Marxist agenda, but this has been in the making for over ninety years. Even small advances can add up to huge advances over long periods of time. An effective Department of Justice (DOJ) and FBI could have stopped this long ago. Unfortunately, even they are now so politicized or shackled with fear of political consequences, they either do nothing or aid the Left. This has allowed the Marxists to progress far more than anyone thought possible. It has even emboldened them to make a big push to complete the job of subduing America quickly. Still, it doesn't take but a few good people in the DOJ and FBI to turn this around and turn back this Marxist aggression.

MARXIST GOAL #20: Infiltrate the press. Get control of book review assignments, editorial writing, and policy making decisions in media.

This is yet another goal the Marxists can check off as completed. Who would have believed that the American news media would become as anti-American, anti-free speech, anti-Christian, and anti-free enterprise as it is today? This did not just happen. It was intentional, well planned, and carried out to undermine the foundations of our democratic Republic.

The primary social media platforms are now some of the most pro-Marxist, anti-free speech organizations to have ever gained a platform and influence in America. They have become steadily more brazen in shutting down any free speech that does not align with their political agenda.

As stated, Marxism is the biggest failure in government and economics in history. And when you dig down just a little into the principles of Marxist government and economics, you don't have to be a genius to see why it has never worked and never can. Thus, a top priority of Marxism is to destroy any free speech or free press that might expose this.

The good news is the American people have not accepted the media and social media's present disdain for truth and freedom of speech. Trust in the media and social media have fallen to all-time lows and are still dropping. When the Biden Administration took office and immediately jerked the nation even harder to the left, the Rasmussen Poll, the most accurate pollster in the last decade, reported that only 23% of Americans thought the nation was going in the right direction.

The American people may have been asleep through much of what the Marxist agenda has done to our country, but there is evidence they are much smarter than our Leftist media thought they were. And now they are beginning to wake up. It doesn't take many to turn back the tide.

MARXIST GOAL #21: Gain control of key positions in radio, TV, and movies.

Once upon a time, Hollywood was a bastion of patriotism honoring American heritage and vehemently resisting Marxism. Until the 1960s, it seemed every movie and television show included a moral lesson, exalted what is good and honorable, and resisted immorality. Then a slow change began. Now they seem resolved to fulfill God's definition of the ultimate corrupt nation as stated in Isaiah 5, to "call evil good, and good evil," to dishonor the honorable and honor the dishonorable.

When a nation stoops to such a level of depravity, God promises through His prophet to judge them with the very things our country now suffers. There are more than a dozen types of judgment in Scripture but only two are condemnation or destruction. The rest are discipline for those the Lord loves. With this increasing judgment on our country, we should be encouraged that it is the disciplinary kind, which is evidence that God still loves us and wants to help us. However, there is a point when debauchery crosses the line and God's only alternative is destruction. We are getting close to that line.

If God did not spare Israel when it was His only representative on earth, we can be sure He will not spare the U.S. or any other country that turns from Him.

We must change course, or we will end up where we are heading—into the deepest darkness and most terrible tyranny the world has known.

How do we change course? By not listening to the media and entertainment which has become a platform for sowing evil and deception into our country and turn back to God who has blessed us so much. Then stand up to the lies and deceptions our media, education system, and arts and entertainment industry have spread about our country and history and stand up for the truth.

MARXIST GOAL #22: Continue discrediting American culture by degrading all forms of artistic expression. Eliminate all good sculpture from parks and buildings and replace with shapeless, awkward, and meaningless forms.

If you have been wondering why art has degenerated into meaningless madness, now you know. Every good thing produced by civilization is a target for Marxist destruction. The quality and message of a nation's art has long been an expression of what is good and true in that nation. Since art is a special custodian of the history and heritage of a nation, it is a Marxist strategy to destroy the arts.

It is the goal of Marxism to destroy the culture, history, heritage, art, uniqueness, and creativity of every nation because they are viewed as primary hindrances to Marxism's unity of conformity, which is their ultimate goal. This includes anything that would project a national identity.

MARXIST GOAL #23: Gain control of art critics and art museum directors and have them promote ugly, repulsive, and meaningless art.

This was obviously meant to fortify and support goal #22. This has been accomplished by the infiltration and near total takeover of education, the media, and arts and entertainment. This is also a large part of "cancel culture" which attacks anything that does not comply with the narrow and shallow mentality of Marxist socialism.

MARXIST GOAL #24: Eliminate all laws governing obscenity by calling them "censorship" and a violation of free speech and freedom of the press.

This is another example of how Marxist strategy uses our laws and Constitution against us. Their promotion of obscenity is to further degrade American culture and morality, which results in the degradation of the nuclear family. Marxists rightly understand the family to be the glue that holds every society together. They also intend to destroy every society and culture and replace it with their own dark version of society, which is nothing less than the slavery of all mankind.

MARXIST GOAL #25: Break down cultural standards of morality by promoting pornography and obscenity in books, magazines, movies, radio, and television.

Marx taught that the family was the biggest rival to the state for the people's allegiance, and so all devotion to family must be destroyed. Marxists also understand that pornography and obscenity are perhaps the most powerful weapons for doing this and therefore devote a great amount of attention to promoting these. This is yet another box Marxists can check since pornography has now crept into nearly every aspect of American life including elementary school textbooks.

MARXIST GOAL #26: Present homosexuality, degeneracy, and promiscuity as "normal, natural, and healthy."

It is counter to the values our American Republic was built on to tolerate any of our fellow citizens being oppressed or discriminated against for race, religion, or even sexual orientation. It is also counter to our culture and values to force or pressure others to accept or adopt what they do not share or agree with. This is now happening in America with sexual orientation. It's not enough to accept the LGBTQ community, we must all celebrate it. This is now being forced in our schools and our military.

This meltdown of morality and sanity in America has now allowed the sowing of gender confusion into elementary school children. The State of Oregon has even passed a law allowing fifteen-year-olds to get sex change surgeries without their parents' consent, paid for by the state! How many fifteen-year-olds are mature and stable enough to make such life-changing decisions? This has nearly always proven to lead to terrible remorse and depression.

It gets worse. It is difficult to even imagine the sickest, most perverted person doing anything worse to our young children than what is now being forced on them in our public schools. As more light is shed on this, some of the horrific stories we will hear will sound too extreme to be true. Yet if this doesn't highlight to us the desperate need for a revolution in education in our country to overthrow these Marxist/socialist perpetrators of such evil, what will?

There is far more to cover on this subject than we can do here. Thankfully, books have and are being written to expose this devastating evil being done to our country, our people, and worst of all our children.

MARXIST GOAL #27: Infiltrate the churches and replace revealed religion with "social" religion. Discredit the Bible and emphasize the need for intellectual maturity which does not need a "religious crutch."

After the family, allegiance to a religion is the most dangerous rival to the Marxist state. Their strategy for weakening Christian faith in America has been effective. Studies have shown that even among the most devout Christian movements, less than 10% now have a biblical worldview. That means at least 90% of those who call and believe themselves to be Christians, now have a worldview fashioned by some other source besides God or the Christian faith.

This explains why the American church has become increasingly ineffective as salt and light and increasingly irrelevant and disrespected by the world. This also explains how a watered-down "social gospel" could replace God's work in the salvation of man with man's works. This is a form of humanism that is counter to true faith. What could more fundamentally replace God's work to save us than man's work to save himself?

Another study showed that only about 10% of those raised in church denominations that claim to be devoted to the Scriptures have been taught the basics of immorality, or what God calls "sin." Still other studies show the moral behavior of Christians in America can no longer be distinguished from non-Christians.

Marx understood that America was built on a Judeo-Christian foundation. Marxists today understand this to be the foundation and strength that enabled America to become the most powerful nation on earth in virtually every major realm of influence. For this reason, they contend if they can destroy the faith of America, they can destroy America. This is another box that is close to being checked.

Resistance to tyranny becomes the Christian and social duty of each individual...Continue steadfast and, with a proper sense of your dependence on God, nobly defend those rights which heaven gave, and no man ought to take from us.

– John Hancock

Chapter 9

Marxist Goals for Destroying America 28 through 32

MARXIST GOAL #28: Eliminate prayer and any type of religious expression in the schools on the grounds it violates the principle of "separation of church and state."

America surrendered to this one far too easily and it has had a devastating impact on our culture. Many believe this to be the single most destructive factor leading to the present meltdown of morality, integrity, and character in America. There is much evidence to support this view. If we had leaders and justices who knew the Constitution and had the integrity and courage to uphold and defend it, this would not have happened in America.

The "separation of church and state" is not found in the Constitution. Anyone who has actually read the Constitution knows this. Again, Marxists are skilled in using propaganda to deceive and promote lies concerning any group in history. Ignorant and inept American leaders and justices have proven to be quick to believe almost anything that is widely spoken or reported in the media as true. Few seem able to even discern between propaganda and truth. For this we can thank our education system which indoctrinates instead of educating and teaching people to think. Our country has paid a terrible price for this incompetence, dereliction of duty, and even collusion with our enemies.

The First Amendment is the only place in our Constitution where the relationship between church and state is addressed, and the statement is clear:

> *Congress shall make no law respecting an establishment of religion, or prohibiting the free exercise thereof.*

The only prohibition in the Constitution for the establishment of religion was for Congress and the federal government, not the states and certainly not the people. The Supreme Court clearly violated this dictate of the Constitution when they outlawed prayer in schools, prohibiting the "free exercise thereof." This has now been expanded to prohibiting prayer nearly everywhere in public—again, a direct violation of the Constitutional mandate.

The Supreme Court also violated the Constitution by allowing the federal government to take authority over state schools. Again, the Constitution is clear: the federal government, which includes the Supreme Court, has no jurisdiction except where specifically given in the Constitution, which this is not.

The Founders also stated in their speeches and personal writings that this clause was to keep the government out of religion, not religion out of the government. In fact, the term "separation of church and state" was first used in

Thomas Jefferson's letter to the Danbury Baptists assuring them the First Amendment was written to keep the federal government out of religion. Again, nowhere is this phrase found in the Constitution or even implied.

The First Amendment also makes clear that only Congress is forbidden to establish religion. It is articulated and understood that the states and people are free to do as they wish regarding religion.

In 1962, the U.S. Supreme Court overturned nearly four hundred years of American tradition and nearly two hundred years of Supreme Court precedents, including the beliefs and practices of our Constitution's Framers. Engel v. Vitale, which forbade prayer in public schools, was one of the most devastating decisions ever by the Supreme Court. The decision not only opened the door wide for the corruption that has since swept over our land but also for the federal government to intrude on the affairs of states and its people, which it had no authority to do except where specifically noted in the Constitution.

Many studies mark the meltdown of morality in America to the date of this decision. This also marked the beginning of the unrelenting attacks on religious liberty in America. What's more, this deeply troubling overreach and unconstitutional Supreme Court decision opened the door for many other decisions that have brazenly ignored and contradicted the Constitution. This released an avalanche by the courts on virtually every right guaranteed by the Bill of Rights as well as the "judicial tyranny" Thomas Jefferson and other Founders considered the greatest threat to our Republic.

Jesus said a tree is known by its fruit. Students can now use the vilest curses freely in school, which is presumed to be protected by First Amendment free speech. However, they can be expelled for using the name of Jesus, which is not presumed to be protected free speech as it should but is instead now stricken by our government. This is a basic revelation of how the government of the most God-loving and God-seeking nation in history has now become anti-religion and antichrist.

The First Amendment protects the foundational freedoms upon which all other freedoms stand. This may be the most powerful forty-five words ever penned to guarantee liberty and is the most powerful counter to the 45 Goals of Marxism for taking over America. So, let's take the one minute it takes to read it in its entirety:

> *Congress shall make no law respecting an establishment of religion, or prohibiting the free exercise thereof; or abridging the freedom of speech, or of the press, or of the right of the people peaceably to assemble, and to petition the government for redress of grievances.*

Marxists know this well: If they can destroy our freedom of religion, freedom of speech, freedom of the press, and right to peaceably assemble, the destruction of all our other freedoms will be quick and easy. Our own Supreme Court has been used for this assault on our most basic freedoms, and if we are ever to reverse this, we must return to the Constitution itself, "the supreme law of the land," a position the Supreme Court has since usurped and claimed for itself.

How could this have happened to us? Through the absence of something we have not had in a long time—leadership with integrity to fulfill the oath to defend the Constitution, first by resolving to know the Constitution, and second by resolving to fight every violation of it, past and present.

MARXIST GOAL #29: Discredit the American Constitution by calling it inadequate, old-fashioned, out-of-step with modern needs, and a hindrance to the cooperation between nations on a worldwide basis.

Of course, the Marxists would promote this belief because they know if they can nullify the Constitution as "the supreme law of the land," they will have destroyed the foundation upon which our Republic stands. Our Republic would be certain to fall. Yet they have been so successful at this our Constitution now hangs by a thread. Without drastic measures, the collapse of our Republic is near.

For any American to so denigrate the Constitution with the argument that it is inadequate is sure evidence they are either ignorant of the Constitution or of American history. They are also ignorant of or complicit with the enemies of our Republic. Our Constitution is our most important government document. It was instrumental in building the most powerful, wealthy, and free country the world has ever known. Next to the Bible, there has been no other document in history that has released as much good onto the world. To call it "inadequate" is the ultimate ignorance or ultimate purposeful betrayal of our country.

To call the Constitution "old fashioned" is even more clear evidence of ignorance or evil intent. Our Constitution was not designed for the culture of the time in which it was written or any other time. It was based on the knowledge of human nature which has been so clearly revealed throughout history. It was brilliantly designed to restrain the evil in men while freeing the good in them. No other document for the establishment of government has been as effective at doing this.

Our Constitution has always been timely because it is based on timeless truths. It is also "self-evident" truth verified repeatedly in the history of mankind, including current events. It is as relevant today as it was when it was first ratified. Perhaps even more so as the evil in man has become increasingly in need of restraint.

Finally, for any American to think that our Constitution is a hindrance to worldwide cooperation is again a revelation in ignorance of both our Constitution and the forces that now shape our world toward ultimate tyranny. Marxism is at the root of globalism and our Constitution is the most powerful bulwark against those seeking to unite the world under this vile tyranny. Our Constitution has and continues to be a basis of cooperation with all other civilized and freedom-loving peoples of the world.

Unfortunately, Marxists understand better how vital the Constitution is to our freedom, prosperity, and strength than most Americans. This must change if we are to continue to exist as a free people.

MARXIST GOAL #30: Discredit the American Founding Fathers as selfish aristocrats who had no concern for "the common man."

The American Founding Fathers were unlike any revolutionaries before or since. It is true they were composed of the wealthiest and most successful people in the colonies, which makes them even more remarkable for leading a revolution. How often do the wealthiest people not just support but lead a revolution? Obviously, this was not done only for their own benefit but to defend and establish the liberty of the common people. This is also why the American Revolution is considered the only truly successful revolution in history and the foundation for the world's longest lasting Republic.

Our Founders should not be discredited for being successful but acknowledged for being nobler than other revolutionaries in history. They had far more if not everything to risk fighting for liberty and the elevation of their fellow citizens. Some gave their lives, others their fortunes, so their fellow citizens could be free. As such, they were the most honorable leading citizens of any country to date.

America's Founding Fathers had flaws like all other men. To state that "all men are created equal" while tolerating slavery is and should be an unforgettable reproach and reminder that even the best among us can have blind spots and collude with evil. This is true of nearly all prominent people past or present. In fact, only one person in history did not have flaws or make mistakes.

Thus, it is important to not only react to the extremes of "cancel culture," but also to acknowledge the mistakes and evils done in our history and learn from them. Still, if we *can* do better, it is not because we *are* better but because we were given the grace to do better by learning from others' mistakes. To think that we are better is pride and a sure way to fall into a worse evil as we are assured in Scripture, **"God resists the proud, but gives grace to the humble" (see James 4:6; I Peter 5:5).**

God's grace is also dependent on obeying the only commandment He gave with a promise: **"Honor your father and mother (which is the first commandment with a promise), so that it may be well with you, and that you may live long on the earth" (Ephesians 6:2-3).** If we want things to go well for us and have longevity, we must honor our national fathers and mothers, not dishonor them. Nowhere does it say we must honor our perfect fathers and mothers because there would be no one to honor. To honor, means to honor the good that they did, but that doesn't mean we cover up their mistakes. The Bible does not cover up even the worst mistakes of its greatest heroes. We must have the maturity and stability to do the same, while always being willing to learn from their mistakes so we don't do the same.

How well has it been going for America since we have allowed this relentless assault on our Founding Fathers and mothers? How could we dishonor them more than to allow lies to displace the truth about them in our history books, then allow our children to be taught those lies? How could we more dishonor them and the grace God bestowed on our country more than to allow what is now being promoted in "cancel culture"?

Isn't it ironic that the same people who attack our Founders for tolerating slavery promote Marxism, the worst form of slavery the world has ever known? This simply affirms what Jesus said: Those who condemn others are guilty of the same (see Matthew 7:3-5). In fact, this may be truer of Marxists than of any other people in history. Everything they condemn in others they perpetrate more than perhaps any other people in history—in racism, in injustice, and in slavery.

Even with our flaws, which can be found in every national heritage, it could be argued that never in human history has such a remarkable group gathered with the level of knowledge, wisdom, truth, and justice like our American Founders. Never has such an elite group stood up to risk so much for the freedom and defense of their fellow citizens.

The Founders of our nation boldly challenged the most powerful empire with the most powerful army and navy in the world when they didn't even have an army or navy. Then, to the astonishment of the whole world, after years of setbacks and terrible defeats, they prevailed. Our freedom did not come cheap and to keep it will not be cheap.

After defeating the British Empire, our Founders were then faced with an even more daunting task—the establishment of a government that could preserve liberty. In this they also prevailed and established a constitution and government like the world had never seen—one devoted to the rights and individual liberties of the common man. Not one place in our Constitution gives preference to the wealthy or powerful.

The Constitution is so extraordinary it was acknowledged around the world as perhaps the most brilliant document, outside of Scripture, ever penned for the benefit of man. Through its brilliance to release stability in government, it aided the advancement of virtually every field of knowledge in a way that had never been seen before.

The application of these brilliant American founding documents was not as brilliant as their writing. It is far easier to see what must be done than to do it. Still, they took a major step in the right direction by ultimately requiring the application of the truths contained therein. It has been a long, arduous process but the Constitution provided a wise procedure to continue with the needed changes to ensure steady progress toward a full application of that vision.

This progress would continue so long as we would continue to adhere to the Constitution. It has only been slowed or stalled when we have ignored the Constitution. The answer to America's problems is not to seek a new Constitution but to comply with the one we already have.

MARXIST GOAL #31: Belittle all forms of American culture and discourage the teaching of American history on the grounds that it was only a minor part of "the big picture."

In this Marxists have realized perhaps their greatest success in corrupting and weakening the youth of our nation. Their strategy to denigrate and destroy has now matured into our current "cancel culture." This movement has manipulated the weak and ignorant into what Scripture calls the ultimate depravity of a nation: calling "evil good, and good evil," or honoring what is dishonorable, while dishonoring what is honorable.

Like all other Marxist lies, they now have many naïve and ignorant Americans believing their own culture and history is the opposite of the truth. America has had one of the most remarkable and honorable histories of any nation. Much the opposite of what revisionist historians have placed in American history textbooks in schools. The true "big picture" is that America has helped lift the entire world to a much higher place than it has ever been in virtually every way.

Again, "Any jackass can kick a barn down, but it takes a skillful carpenter to build one." Marxism only tears down and destroys, which has been proven historically in every country subjected to it. Americans, on the other hand, have built more substance and benefit to the world than any other nation. America has not been perfect but far better than what is being taught to our children today by revisionist historians, and far better than what has been projected by our media, arts, and entertainment.

MARXIST GOAL #32: Support socialist movements that give centralized control to any part of culture— education, social agencies, welfare programs, mental health clinics, etc.

In this also Marxists have been successful. Since virtually all American culture is now being centrally controlled by the federal government, we are now fundamentally controlled by a "deep state" bureaucracy that is fundamentally Leftist and Marxist. This explains why our federal government now supports anti-American trends and policies.

The "deep state" is composed of an estimated three- million bureaucrats in our federal government who have been given more power to micromanage America through regulation than it could be argued Congress has by passing legislation.

That power was given to the bureaucrats by our Supreme Court which, again, in direct conflict with the Constitution, gave regulations written by bureaucrats the power of law. The Constitution clearly states only Congress can make laws.

These unconstitutional laws in the form of bureaucratic regulations have become increasingly intrusive in controlling even the smallest details of our lives. Such laws are not only being written by unelected bureaucrats but also without checks or balances, the Constitutional basis for restraining unbridled abuse of power. As expected, the worst abuses of power are now coming from this bureaucracy. Because of this one incomprehensible and unconstitutional decision by the Supreme Court, we are daily losing our freedom and strength as a nation.

Winston Churchill foresaw giant government bureaucracies as a threat to liberty and to civilization itself. His prophecy is now being fulfilled, but that does not mean we cannot resist and turn it back.

The liberties of our country, the freedom of our civil Constitution, are worth defending at all hazards; and it is our duty to defend them against all attacks. We have received them as a fair inheritance from our worthy ancestors. They purchased them for us with toil and danger at the expense of treasure and blood, and transmitted them to us with care and diligence. It will bring an everlasting mark of infamy on the present generation, enlightened as it is, if we should suffer them to be wrested from us by violence without a struggle, or to be cheated out of them by the artifices of false and designing men.

– Samuel Adams, called "The Father of the American Revolution."

Chapter 10

Marxist Goals for Destroying America 33 through 39

MARXIST GOAL #33: Eliminate all laws and procedures which interfere with the operation of the communist apparatus.

The goal of the "communist apparatus" is to condition the population for totalitarian control. One method used against Americans is called "tyranny of the minority." This is done by passing laws or court orders to appease a tiny minority of the population who claim to be offended thereby limiting or canceling the rights of the majority.

To be a great nation, we should want to protect minorities as much as possible from abuse, threats, or unnecessary offenses of any kind except where those protections inhibit or destroy everyone else's freedom and rights. Today, people can claim to be offended by just about anything. However, in so doing, our population is being conditioned to think that offending someone is the worst possible, sickening crime. Instead, we should be far more sickened by those who are using this deception to create a far greater division between people groups, while stealing our liberties and freedom of speech.

As this conditioning of our population plays itself out, its ultimate power play is to destroy freedom of speech by making "hate speech" a federal crime. America has already fallen to unprecedented madness by exalting someone's temporary emotions to determine if they are male, female, or some invented gender. How many young men in high school do you think will "feel" female when it's time to shower in the girls' gym class? We already have men claiming to "feel like a woman" so they can compete in women's sports. This will not only destroy women's sports, but it will also destroy our society.

This level of sickness is beyond where any nation in history has fallen. Just think of the implications of male prison inmates claiming to "feel like females" so they can get transferred to women's prisons. How has America become so docile to such madness? We have been conditioned not to offend anyone's feelings lest we be called a racist, bigot, or worse. Just being accused of these can now come with penalties like losing your job, being ostracized by your profession or society, or even violence.

Consider the ramifications of allowing someone's claimed feelings to take precedence over clear physical evidence to the contrary. It's time for America to be offended by the insanity our leadership has led us into. We must always be devoted to protecting the weak, oppressed, and minorities from true attacks, but we also need also to be offended by those who use their minority status to dominate the majority and steal our liberties.

This is the same strategy Marxists use to break up families, churches, and all other close relationships that are deemed as threats to people's unquestioning allegiance to the state. The whole world is marveling at the insanity and moral depravity this cultural meltdown in America now demonstrates. Has any society ever gone this crazy this fast? What will it take for us to wake up and take back what has been stolen from us?

The Marxist strategy for conditioning us has been for a minority to claim to be offended by something, then call anyone a "racist" who protests this overreaction to appease a handful of people. The truth is, if we have not been called a "racist" by someone or some group, we are not engaged, as we should be, in this culture war that seeks to enslave America. Anyone who cowers before this threat of being labeled a racist is allowing evil to prevail and is not fit to be a leader in this or any other nation.

MARXIST GOAL #34: Eliminate the House Committee on Un-American Activities (HCUA).

This is yet another goal the Marxists can mark as accomplished. How it was done so fast and easily is a revelation in how foolish, naïve, and inept we Americans have been to recognize and counter such attacks. Not only has the elimination of the HCUA been accomplished but this committee which was once an effective bulwark against Nazism and Marxism is so demeaned, the HCUA itself is now considered unamerican and a national embarrassment. Here are just a few facts that revisionist historians do not want you to know:

1. Senator Joseph McCarthy's hearings rocked the nation by unmasking communist spies at some of the highest levels of government, including a Secretary of State and other centers of influence in society. Yet he was ultimately driven from office in shame with accusations of having falsely accused some. However, when the Iron Curtain fell and KGB files were opened to the West, it was discovered that every person McCarthy named as a spy was, in fact, a KGB spy.

2. President John F. Kennedy was a close friend of Senator McCarthy. Their families vacationed together. President Kennedy considered McCarthy's work vital to defending America by exposing Marxist infiltrators. Today, Kennedy remains the staunchest anti-Marxist President of either party next to Ronald Reagan.

3. The Marxist strategy to destroy the HCUA was inevitable since it had previously been effective in thwarting the entire Marxist strategy for taking over America. Since the HCUA was disbanded, Marxists have made swift progress in accomplishing their goal of dismantling the American Republic.

As this Marxist strategy becomes more clearly illuminated, we can see their success in revising our history so that the good seem evil and the evil become heroes. Thus, as we dig down into the histories published before this massive assault, we find that many who have been made villains by the present narrative were actually heroes. This is especially true since many of those vilified were effective in exposing the Marxist agenda. So now they are being marginalized and their reputations destroyed.

Knowing this, to be a true freedom fighter and to stand against this great darkness of Marxism, we must value our country far more than we value our own reputation. If we are not being attacked, called racists, bigots, phobes, and every other form of character attack, we are not really in the fight. When you start taking flak (antiaircraft fire) it is because you are over the target. We must consider every attack a call to become more focused and resolute. Quitting is not an option.

MARXIST GOAL #35: Discredit and eventually dismantle the FBI.

Under its founder, J. Edgar Hoover, the FBI became the most effective and respected law enforcement agency in the world. It was also the most effective at countering both Nazi and Marxist insurgencies. Immediately after Hoover died and could no longer defend himself, an onslaught of accusations about him and the FBI were spread by the media. However, the integrity of the FBI was so high at the time little damage had been done to the FBI. This changed the strategy of Marxists and Islamists to one of infiltration.

Recent revelations of political bias and widespread corruption in the FBI have made it clear: The FBI and DOJ are now controlled by the "deep state." Instead of fighting Marxism, they are now defending and even promoting

Marxism. This has been one of the most important of all Marxist goals accomplished, and one of the most threatening to our freedoms.

The integrity and political neutrality of such a powerful agency as the FBI is essential. Recent exposure of the politicization and weaponization at the top of the FBI is more than troubling; it has been called treason and for good reason. So far, changes made at the top to counter this corruption have revealed even deeper levels of corruption. Some are now suggesting the corruption is so widespread the FBI must be dismantled, and its mission given to another agency such as the U.S. Marshals.

Another option would be to create a new agency with new leadership. That may be necessary, but that could set back federal law enforcement for years if not decades. The FBI has been one of the most effective defenses against domestic threats to our Republic, so rooting out this corruption must be a top priority. If this crucial law enforcement agency is not swept clean and restored to the unbiased force for justice it once was, what has been one of our most powerful weapons against our enemies could become one of our worst enemies within.

MARXIST GOAL #36: Infiltrate and gain control of unions.

As early as the 1930s, there were concerns if America took sides against Stalinist Russia, the unions might shut down supply transportation needed for our defense. Some think we remain in such a precarious position today or worse. Not only do Marxists and Marxist sympathizers now control many of our unions, some of these unions are also vital to our national defense. What's more, crucial materials and electronic chips for our nuclear weapons are manufactured in Communist China.

When these Marxist goals for destroying America were formulated, the great majority of union leaders and members were staunch anti-Marxists and American patriots. Many and perhaps most union members still are. Even so, many unions, including some of the most powerful, have been infiltrated and taken over by Marxist operatives.

Two of the most powerful unions in America that have moved in near lockstep with the Marxist agenda are the teachers' unions and public service unions. Marxist operatives in the teachers' unions have inserted Marxist indoctrination into public school curricula. The public service unions have served as inroads to the "deep state," which is an immediate threat to our Constitutional Republic.

Until recently perhaps, President Franklin Roosevelt was the most pro-socialist and pro-union Chief Executive to occupy the White House. Even he was vehemently against unions being formed for federal employees, calling this a basic threat to our security. He was right. The now very powerful public service unions are considered one of the greatest threats to our country's security. How could this happen? Again, the election and appointment of weak, naïve, and inept leadership in our government who obviously cared more about their own positions than our future.

Other unions that represent a potential security threat to our nation include those in a position to shut down needed defense and high priority supplies such as food, medicine, and a huge part of all commerce in America. With the FBI now so compromised that some of its leaders would develop plans to overthrow a duly elected President, we can no longer trust them to guard us.

While we must understand how serious this threat is to our national and domestic security, we must not forget that some unions have had a positive impact on American workers and America. They have played a major role in bettering wages, benefits, and work and safety conditions. However, this Marxist goal of taking over unions is for other purposes, which have been achieved in some unions. Many union members remain patriotic Americans. Nevertheless, Marxist indoctrination of union workers continues, and the threat of this continues to grow.

MARXIST GOAL #37: Infiltrate and gain control of big business.

One great misunderstanding that many Americans have is Republicans are for big business, Democrats are for the workers and common people. However, if we look at actions and policies and not just rhetoric, we will see that Republicans have done far more for common people and small businesses, while the Democrats have recently sided far more with big business. As with most other Marxist goals, Americans have been conditioned to believe propaganda even when facts prove otherwise.

For example, Democratic Presidential candidates have continually run on the platform of being against the oppression of big business and monopolies yet do nothing to challenge them when in office. Therefore, big business and monopolies tend to support Democratic candidates over Republicans. It was Republican President Teddy Roosevelt who took on the big railroad, steel, and energy monopolies and broke them up. This had to be done to keep competition in American business from being crushed. He also passed the first antitrust laws, accomplishing what Democrats had promised to do for decades.

Democrats siding with big business continues to this day. During the Obama Administration, small community banks were nearly destroyed when President Obama sided with the big banks after the 2008 subprime mortgage crisis, even though the big banks created the crisis. Obama claimed he was doing this for the good of the people, but it did not work out that way.

Likewise, the Democratic Party has given lip service to the African-American community for nearly three quarters of a century, yet has done nothing to improve the condition of their community in any measurable way. The Democratic Party claims to represent the interests of the "little guy." They do this by keeping them "little," so they can keep their vote. They know that if a minority breaks out of its government-imposed poverty, they will see the light, and many will become Republicans.

Just as Marxist propaganda is the opposite of Marxist reality, the rhetoric of the Democratic Party remains the opposite of their practice. Many Republicans do the same. Still, the policies and practices of the Democratic Party overwhelmingly side with big business. Only Republicans have successfully challenged big business and consistently aided small businesses and average Americans.

By its nature, the Left is for consolidation which leads to centralization and puts the accumulation of power and wealth into the hands of the few. That is essentially Marxism. Thus, as the influence of Marxism grows in the Democratic Party, they increasingly promote big government, big business, and big banks.

The Carter Administration once implied that small businesses made up only about 6% of the American economy. When challenged on this, they did a study to determine just what that number was. To their shock and virtually everyone else's, they learned that small businesses composed at least 50% of the American economy. A "small business" in that study was defined as having twenty-five employees or less. Had they used what is generally considered a small business, fifty employees or less, this percentage would have been far higher.

It is big business that makes up the smaller percentage of the economy. In this same study, it was also learned that 75% to 80% of all new jobs were created by these small businesses. Again, if they had used a definition of fifty employees or less this number could have been 90% or higher.

Under the Obama Administration, growth in the American economy slowed to less than 1% a year. President Obama said this was the "new norm," and that we should expect this in the future. That would no doubt have been true had Democrats remained in power since their policies are damaging to small businesses—the key to economic growth and health in America. There was laughter and scorn when President Trump said the economy could reach 5% annual growth, until it did in just two years under his administration. Because his policies helped the "little guy," the unemployment rate of every racial and economic subgroup also fell to dramatic levels—something Obama said not to expect again.

If we are to escape the threatened Marxist takeover of our country, we must learn that Marxist, Leftist propaganda is the opposite of their true intent. Remember when President Obama said the federal government would never get into the automobile business, then seized control of General Motors that same afternoon? Remember when he said under the Affordable Care Act the cost of health insurance would go down and we could keep our present policies and doctors? The result was the opposite. We could cite many more examples, but the question remains: How long will it be before we wake up and realize what is being done to us?

Have the Republicans done any better? Occasionally, a little. In truth, both political parties have led us to this present crisis. Perhaps we should heed George Washington's warning that we have no political parties in America, since they only seem to result in foolish, incompetent people running our government. As our first President asserted, we should debate all issues as Americans and not allow political parties to drive us again to where we now find ourselves.

MARXIST GOAL #38: Transfer some of the powers of arrest from the police to social agencies. Treat all behavioral problems as psychiatric disorders which only psychiatrists can understand or treat.

Both Darwin's and Freud's theories were embraced by Marx since both confirmed his premise that the state needed to control humanity. Thus, psychiatry and psychoanalysis have become primary weapons for Marxists to achieve their goals. Freudian psychiatry, for example, is used by Marxists to achieve their goal of breaking up the family structure and anything else that could rival the state as a source of people's authority and allegiance.

This is not to imply that all psychology, psychiatry, or psychoanalysis is Marxist. However, they have become primary tools for Marxists to subjugate the people they conquered.

MARXIST GOAL #39: Dominate the psychiatric profession and mental health laws as a means of gaining coercive control over those who oppose Marxist goals.

They may do this gradually, but Marxists will eventually declare as insanity any belief that challenges Marxist doctrine or the supremacy of the state. They use insane asylums and labor camps to banish those who hold such beliefs to reindoctrinate them or work them to death. Fear of being declared insane is a primary and effective tool of the Marxist state.

As this strategy developed, behavioral drugs, shock treatments, and many other forms of torture were added. Some Marxist states have even eclipsed the Nazis and the horrors of the Inquisition in the Middle Ages in cruelty to their own people. If anyone subjected to a state mental institution survived, they would often be maimed for life—body, soul, and spirit.

Likewise, those who embrace Marxism take on a most demented insanity as Marx did. Since power is concentrated to a few Marxist elites, the principle of corruption by power is concentrated and magnified. For example, when Stalin began withholding food and basic needs from people that he considered noncompliant, thousands died. But their small number of protests encouraged him to go further. Before long, tens of millions were being expunged in this way, and this was perfectly acceptable to Marxist leaders.

The demented thinking of those who are addicted to power can quickly grow into cruel insanity. This happened with some church leaders in the Dark Ages, it happened with the Nazis, but the Marxists' evil insanity remains the deadliest and cruelest of all.

All political power comes from the barrel of a gun. The communist party must command all the guns, that way no guns can ever be used to command the party.

– Mao Zedong

❧ Chapter 11 ❦

Marxist Goals for Destroying America 40 through 45

MARXIST GOAL #40: Discredit the family as an institution. Encourage promiscuity and easy divorce.

As we have seen, many of these goals overlap and expand on previous goals. Since the family was seen as a primary rival for the allegiance of the people, promoting promiscuity and easy divorce became effective weapons for destroying the family.

As reported in *The Naked Communist* (p. 133), Marxists have been very effective in accomplishing this goal as well. From 1958 to 1990, the divorce rate in America increased by over 100%. The reason the divorce rate has since flattened is even more disturbing—fewer people are getting married, choosing to cohabitate instead. In 1958, the cohabitation rate in America was near zero. Today, more couples do this than get married. As an increasing percentage of children are born out of wedlock, the next Marxist goal becomes even more easily achievable.

MARXIST GOAL #41: Emphasize the need to raise children away from the negative influence of parents. Attribute prejudices, mental blocks, and mentally retarded children to the suppressive influence of parents.

It is basic Marxist doctrine that children belong to the state, not their parents. Marxists quickly seized upon Freud's theories attributing almost all mental disorders and depression to what he considered an archaic family structure and parents imposing Dark Age beliefs and morals on their children.

Once goal #38 is achieved giving arresting powers to social services and Marxists establish that any deviation from Marxist doctrine is a form of insanity, parents are arrested, or children are seized and made wards of the state or both.

In Europe and America, all these goals have been used to attack and destroy families and have been so successful that strong families have become an increasing rarity. Subtly worded bills have been proposed in the U.S. Congress which would make devotion to family, political conservativism, or religious devotion, recognized forms of insanity for the purpose of removing children from homes.

If you don't think this can happen here, just think how fast this present moral and social corruption has come on our nation. Such forms of legislation have already been passed, in some cases, by being inserted into healthcare laws. Such legislation also denies our Constitutional rights and usurps increasing totalitarian control over our lives. All this is being achieved faster and easier than most thought possible.

MARXIST GOAL #42: Create the impression that violence and insurrection are legitimate aspects of American tradition; that students and special interest groups should rise and use "united force" to solve economic, political, or social problems.

Does this sound like the rationale being used for the recent and present insurrections, violence, and attacks on public and private property in American universities and cities? Does this sound like the excuses the Democratic Party has recently used to refuse to condemn and instead to justify such violence? This is yet another example of how effective Marxists have been at infiltrating and sowing discord into our schools, politics, and our country.

We can also see the hypocrisy of the Democratic Party to quickly label any protest done by conservatives as "insurrection" or "treason." Media coverage and skewed polls make it sound like most Americans agree with these labels—they do not.

Polls can be made to say anything by who and how the questions are asked. We saw this when Wikileaks exposed Hillary Clinton's emails. Pollsters were asking the Clinton campaign what they wanted the polls to say. We should know this well after the last two decades that polls no longer accurately reflect people's preferences. Instead, they are now used as political weapons.

Studies continue to show about a third of Americans are hard left and will believe anything the Leftist media propagates. The other two-thirds of Americans are not so naïve or slow of reasoning and increasingly doubt Leftist propaganda and the media. In fact, the media has now fallen below Congress as being the least trusted by the American people. Americans have now joined more than 80% of the world who do not trust their media.

Still, the third of Americans who are on the Left are now hard left and are becoming increasingly radicalized and mobilized. This way, they can make enough noise to seem bigger than they really are. Still, their smaller numbers don't make them any less dangerous. Let's not forget Lenin and the Bolsheviks numbered less than 1% of the Russian population when they began their revolution, and they succeeded. How did they do this with such a tiny percentage of the population?

1. By forming alliances with other liberal and anti-Tsarist groups that thought they could control the Marxists and keep them in their place after the revolution was won. Unfortunately, these groups were completely unprepared for the ruthlessness of the Marxists and did not have the courage to stand against them when they could easily had beaten them.

2. By promising amnesty to all soldiers and citizens who would surrender their weapons. Once the army and citizenry had disarmed, the Bolsheviks killed millions who could no longer protect themselves, including the leaders and members of the other liberal groups that had aided them in the revolution. Thus, having rid the country of all potential rivals, they could quickly and easily establish totalitarian control.

This strategy for disarming the people before a great purge worked so well in Russia it has been repeated in many other countries the Marxists have subdued. Will

America become their next victim? We will if we let them take our weapons.

MARXIST GOAL #43: Overthrow all dictatorships before native populations are ready for self-government.

As we have seen, Marxist goals applied to democratic governments where people are more independent is patient and methodical as they seek to undermine and destroy the foundations of democracy and freedom. Where there are dictatorships, Marxists have been quicker to advocate revolution as dictators are usually hated by the people subjected to them. As bad as some dictators have been, few are as bad as a Marxist dictatorship.

MARXIST GOAL #44: Internationalize the Panama Canal.

President Jimmy Carter fell headlong for this one and gave up one of the most strategic passageways in the world to a company owned by Communist China. The U.S. treaty with Panama that allowed the U.S. to build and control the canal "in perpetuity" was abrogated by the Carter Administration for no apparent reason. The Chinese now control it, not only to our peril, but to that of the world.

MARXIST GOAL #45: Repeal the Connally Reservation so the U.S. cannot prevent the World Court from seizing

jurisdiction over U.S. domestic issues. Give the World Court Jurisdiction over nations and individuals alike.

Since Marxists gained control of the United Nations and thereby the World Court, it has understandably been eager to pass laws in the U.S. Congress which would recognize the authority of the World Court over American citizens. This would abolish the U.S. Constitution as "the supreme law of the land" and make every U.S. citizen subject to prosecution by the World Court.

The current primary objective of the international body aimed at this goal is to cancel the Second Amendment of the U.S. Constitution making it illegal for its citizens to have arms. Since the 1917 Bolshevik Revolution in Russia, Marxists have learned that disarming citizens is crucial to subjugating and pacifying a population.

So far, resistance to this has been one of the few remaining lynchpins of resistance to Marxism in America. We pray these weapons never get used for this purpose, but just having them can be a major deterrent. Therefore, confiscating weapons remains a top Marxist priority for America.

Neither Japan nor Germany had plans for invading America in World War II, largely because both thought it to be impossible with so many of its citizens being armed. This is also one reason Germany did not invade Switzerland even when they controlled all other surrounding countries. Swiss citizens are required to be a part of the national militia and to have arms and ammunition in their homes in case of a national emergency. Consequently, there is little crime in Switzerland.

It is no coincidence that the cities in America with the strongest gun control laws also have the highest crime rates. Criminals don't obey laws. Gun control laws only disarm law-abiding citizens and make them more vulnerable.

The American Founders made it clear the main reason for the Second Amendment to the Constitution and the right of every American citizen to bear arms was to defend ourselves against our own government should it become tyrannical. Now that Marxists/socialists are close to seizing control of our government, both legislative and executive orders are being proposed which, if passed, would threaten our most basic First and Second Amendment rights. This is why Americans have been arming like never in our history. American citizens may appear docile for a time, but there is an obvious awakening happening. We will not be easily subdued.

No American citizen should want to or need to rise against their own government, but when it has been subdued and is being controlled by those who threaten its liberty and continued existence as a Republic, there comes a time when true patriots who love their country, families, and fellow citizens must rise.

Another important reason for all Americans to consider being armed is the increasingly lawlessness in our country. Multitudes of violent gang members and terrorists have been pouring across our southern border. This combined with the Marxist agenda to defund and neutralize our police is a recipe for disaster. If we love our families, neighbors, and country, we must be prepared to help defend them.

Any power must be an enemy of mankind which enslaves the individual by power and by force, whether it arises under the Fascist or the Communist flag. All that is valuable in human society depends upon the opportunity for development accorded to the individual.

– Albert Einstein

❧ Chapter 12 ❧

Battle Stations

The Call to Action

When we look at the infiltration of Marxism into American government and culture and how far they have progressed toward their goal of destroying the American Republic, it may seem like their success is inevitable. It is not. However, what we can deduce is that Marxists care more about destroying our Republic than Americans seem to care about preserving it. When this reverses, victory over Marxism will be certain.

Marxists now have America in its most desperate struggle for survival since the American Revolution. However, Marxism is also now in its place of greatest vulnerability. Or as one courageous World War II American general responded when told they were surrounded by the enemy, "Great! Attack in all directions. They won't get away this time!" This may be our most desperate hour, but it is also theirs. We now have a real chance to drive this evil completely from our land.

As one of our more brilliant Founders, Thomas Jefferson declared, "All tyranny needs to gain a foothold is for people of good conscience to remain silent." We can now attest to this truth. By being complacent, the worst evil mankind has ever faced now has far more than a foothold in our land.

Still, as Earl Taylor, Jr., President of the National Center for Constitutional Studies, predicted about how Jefferson's statement could come to pass and be overcome:

Jefferson then explained why we should not lose hope—even when we see our elected officials beginning to abandon the Constitution. Ultimately, he said, the people themselves will restore America to its founding principles.

Jefferson was right. It will not be our elected officials who will save us; it will be *the people*. When we the American people wake up to what is being done to us, take up this fight that our elected officials have cowered before and take back our land, we will have a new breed of leadership elected to our government.

In our Republic, the people are the sovereign, not the elected officials. Elected officials work for us (though most seem to have long forgotten this). Our government, having been taken over and run by politicians instead of statesmen, has run our ship of state aground. Our government is now in the hands of politicians, which our government was never designed to allow. It may now be incapable of fixing itself, but the people are beginning to wake up and take back their government. The calls for a second American Revolution to restore what was established by the first are growing.

We can thank the Marxists for waking us up to the tragedy of what has become our government, originally established to be "of the people, for the people, by the people." The insidious plans that Marxists have for our destruction is now being exposed in books, articles, talk shows and has become one of the hottest topics in America. More importantly, the American people are starting to fight back.

Marxism has been able to destroy many nations because it has a clear purpose and strategy. Marxists have been wiser than Western leaders. They understand Marxism cannot coexist with freedom or any democratic form of government. And now the American people are waking up to this same reality. Freedom and democracy cannot coexist with Marxism and therefore Marxism must be driven from our land.

Abraham Lincoln once said, if the American Republic was ever destroyed it would not come from an external enemy but from enemies within. Now his prophetic wisdom is obvious. We now face the greatest threat to our continued existence, and it has come from our fellow Americans who have embraced this Marxist delusion. Our fellow Americans are being used to spread this Marxist poison among us. More are beginning to acknowledge we are already in a second American civil war. We are because wars are not always physical.

Economic and cultural wars have accomplished some of the greatest geopolitical changes in history. It is not wrong to hope the present conflict can be won without violence or without more violence. Our goal should be to convert our misled fellow Americans, not kill them.

At the same time, "If we do not change our direction we will end up where we are headed," and where we are headed would lead to increasing violence.

While it is right to seek to restrain violence as much as possible, it now seems likely we will experience more violence than we have in any previous conflict. Therefore, we hope and work for the best, while we prepare for the worst. This conflict will not be settled without the removal of Marxism from our land, or it will have victory over us. As increasing tensions make clear, one way or the other this will be settled soon.

We cannot defeat an enemy we cannot see. We must first identify the enemy, then resolve to let them either surrender their Marxist agenda that is contrary to all that America is and was and become loyal Americans, or they will no longer have a place in our land.

To date, every time Marxism has been defeated or pushed back, even in the former Soviet Union, it only retreated far enough to regroup and come back more powerful, deceptive, and deadlier than ever. Only the complete eradication of Marxism from the earth will spell victory. We cannot accept less. Marxism is a spirit of death and will continue to be so long as we tolerate its existence. We cannot continue to accept small victories; we must destroy it.

This does not mean destroy all Marxists. Many will wake up to the deception when this conflict heats up. Our goal should be to deliver them from what deceived them and set them free from this most deadly, terrible yoke of slavery. The truth spoken in love with clarity, conviction, and resolve has the power to do this.

With a couple of exceptions, the world has been incomprehensibly weak in its response to Marxism. Since it is now more powerful than ever, we are likely entering a confrontation in which many on both sides will perish before this great evil can be eradicated from the earth. However, far more will perish if Marxism is allowed to remain. It is a spirit of death.

Now that we know the truth about Marxism, not what its propagandists say, we can see that it is far deadlier than the worst plague or any other calamity the world has suffered. It is a social pandemic and deadly disease that must be eradicated. To do so, we must educate everyone on what Marxism truly is, stripping it of its most powerful weapons—deception and propaganda.

The Deceivers are Deceived

Marxism abides in such darkness that few Marxist operatives even know what it is. Most of them have been persuaded by propaganda and few investigate any deeper. The same is true of those who have been seduced by wayward religious convictions that are without scriptural basis. Charles Spurgeon said he could find ten men who would die for the Bible for every one that would read it. We can have all the religious zeal in the world, but we too can be deceived if we don't read the book!

I know this is true about Marxists because I once was one. I had superficial motives, as is the case with many. I became suspicious when I realized Marxist rhetoric did not match Marxist realities in every country they took over. I started reading everything Marx and other Marxist leaders had written and quickly realized what was being promoted as the "hope of mankind" was more like what is portrayed in George Orwell's *1984* and *Animal Farm*, only much worse!

Many Marxists are idealists who think they are doing something good for mankind. They think Marxism is the only remedy to many of our problems. Many of them do not have evil intent. They just don't understand what's really behind the seemingly great and idealistic cause they promote. Marxism's goal is to destroy the best civilization ever produced and replace it with the worst tyranny ever devised.

The Undeceived Deceivers

True Marxists, the ones who know what they are doing and promoting, have little respect for the idealists who are so easily manipulated. They may pretend to have great respect for them because they know idealists, especially the ones who fashion themselves as intellectuals, are easily controlled simply by massaging their egos. Still, true Marxists only have contempt and disdain for idealists, which is why they refer to them as "useful idiots." This is also why they are often the first to be killed or sent to labor camps when Marxists seize control of a country.

Marxist propaganda, on the other hand, projects nothing but care for human rights, fairness, justice, and equality. But a true Marxist really doesn't care about any of those things and has nothing but contempt for them. True Marxists hate idealistic Marxists because they know true Marxism is not idealism; it's propaganda. In true Marxism, the only thing that matters is control, making people compliant and obedient.

Deception and façade permeate Marxism. Consequently, Marxists have been able to enter and control nearly every center of influence in the West from government to social clubs. They quickly build friendships and form alliances with emerging high-impact people who can help them gain access to organizations and clubs where the wealthy and powerful gather.

Marxists have even developed some of their own organizations to attract such influencers. Until one truly understands Marxism and its strategy, it is nearly impossible to expose the roots and purposes of these organizations, but once one sees the true nature of Marxism, the Marxist influence in these organizations becomes obvious.

This is not speculation. Many Marxists have written books about this. Their true intentions are clear in their 45- part plan for destroying America. As Terence McKenna said, "The problem is not to find the answer; it's to face the answer."

The Great Conundrum

The terrible irony is Lincoln had to fight a civil war to save the Union. We now find ourselves in a similar predicament. Though it is right to hope this is settled in the least deadly and destructive way possible, what looms over us now could be far deadlier and destructive than even our Civil War. Nevertheless, if we must fight, even a civil war, we must resolve to win it. How?

In our War of Independence and the Civil War, two of America's greatest leaders emerged to navigate us through those times. This is called "the grace of God." As Scripture attests, the first evidence of God's favor on a nation is wise leaders. The first evidence of God's judgment on a nation is immature, capricious leaders (see Isaiah Chapters 1-5).

What we face now seems more difficult than what Washington or Lincoln faced. Yet God always seems to do His best work when the odds are the greatest—nothing is impossible with God! We may be in over our heads, and we will not get through this without His help. Still, our country was founded on a battle that could not be won without God's help. Fighting against great odds is our DNA! The same God who promised to complete the good work He began in us (see Philippians 1:6) always finishes what He starts. In this we can trust.

Not only can we survive these overwhelming odds, but we can also use this present conflict to restore our Republic to the great and strong foundations this most powerful and prosperous nation in history was built on. Our Constitution is the most powerful document ever composed for establishing a wise, righteous, and just government and for defending freedom, justice, and basic human dignity. It is all we need if we adhere to it, but we must restore its moorings which are so weakened they have now nearly completely severed.

As remarkable as the U.S. Constitution is, it has never fully been adhered to. It has never fully been "the supreme law of the land" as sanctioned. In fact, we have rarely complied with our Constitution. This failure may be the root of our great social fault lines and divisions to this day. If we had begun by fully complying with the Constitution, this would have deprived the Marxists and all other enemies of the oxygen they now thrive on, compliments of our governing injustices and inconsistencies.

Again, we can have the best form of government and still have bad government if we don't put good people in it. Our Republic has not failed, we have failed. We have failed by ignoring the warnings of Washington, Jefferson, Adams, Franklin, Lincoln, and otherwise leaders America has been blessed with like Daniel Webster, George Washington Carver, Thomas Sowell, and many others. Their warnings must be revisited, so we do not repeat history's mistakes and suffer the same terrible consequences.

If we have the capacity to humble ourselves and learn from our mistakes, we can use this whole experience, even all the civil conflict now upon us to restore our foundations and fortify ourselves against all enemies foreign and domestic. This present battle may lead to the greatest nation on earth rising to even greater heights and helping the rest of the world to do the same.

To prevail in this present conflict, we must be like the inhabitants of Jerusalem in Nehemiah's time, rebuilding the walls that protect us with a trowel in one hand and a sword in the other. We must learn to build and fight at the same time. We must teach this basic concept in all our schools and to every American, so this never happens to us again.

The purpose of this book is to illuminate Marxism and its strategies and tactics for dismantling the American Republic and what is left of Western civilization. This includes how we have never lived up to our Constitution and founding documents, and the subsequent troubles and opportunities for evil we have brought on ourselves.

Even if we can defeat and push back Marxism from our land, we cannot just go back to where we were before this battle. If we do, we will certainly have to fight it again. We must dig deeper by adhering to our remarkable foundations as a nation and building upon them with wisdom and fidelity to the truth, which all the lessons of history teach. To do this, we must resolve to not only be a nation with a great vision of liberty and justice for all, but to also be a nation where these truths are lived without compromise.

Rebellion to tyrants is obedience to God.

– Thomas Jefferson

ADVENTURE
❧ AWAITS ❧

NEW RELEASES AND CLASSICS
BY RICK JOYNER

FIND THESE AND MORE ON THE WEBSTORE
AT WWW.MSTARM.ORG/STORE

MorningStar
PARTNERS

Our MorningStar Partners have grown into an extraordinary global fellowship of men and women who are committed to seeing The Great Commission fulfilled in our times. Join us in equipping the body of Christ through conferences, schools, media, and publications.

We are committed to multiplying the impact of the resources entrusted to us. Your regular contribution of any amount—whether it's once a month or once a year—will make a difference!

In His Service,

PARTNER WITH US TODAY